PREMENSTRUAL SYNDROME

The Essential Guide

Susie
Perry Debice

Premenstrual Syndrome – The Essential Guide is also available in accessible formats for people with any degree of visual impairment. The large print edition and eBook (with accessibility features enabled) are available from Need2Know. Please let us know if there are any special features you require and we will do our best to accommodate your needs.

First published in Great Britain in 2012 by
Need2Know
Remus House
Coltsfoot Drive
Peterborough
PE2 9BF
Telephone 01733 898103
Fax 01733 313524
www.need2knowbooks.co.uk

Contents

Introduction 5

Chapter 1 **What is PMS?**.................................7

Chapter 2 **Your 28-Day Cycle** 15

Chapter 3 **PMS Symptoms**...............................29

Chapter 4 **PMS Profiles** 43

Chapter 5 **Hormone Imbalance**.........................53

Chapter 6 **Diet and Lifestyle Factors**...........65

Chapter 7 **Good Nutrition**................................79

Chapter 8 **Natural Therapies and Remedies**..........95

Chapter 9 **Stress and PMS**..............................115

Chapter 10 **Seven Steps to Beating PMS** 123

Chapter 11 **Recipes**...135

Help List 147

Introduction

Did you know that there are over 100 recorded symptoms associated with PMS? That's a staggering amount! No wonder women all over the world experience different types of PMS. These symptoms are grouped into physical or emotional and behavioral categories, and occur due to different types of hormone imbalance.

During the early chapters of this book you'll be guided through a series of questionnaires and action points that will help you get to know your own type of PMS. You'll get a better understanding of your cycle, you'll discover your core and associated symptoms, you'll work out your unique PMS profile and you'll uncover the type of hormone imbalance driving your PMS forward.

Once you have all this information to hand, you can start to think about why you have ended up suffering from PMS. There are lots of different triggers associated with PMS, including hormone imbalance, poor diet, lack of exercise, stress and conditions such as constipation, underactive thyroid and poor liver function. Not to mention drinking too much alcohol and having a toxic lifestyle. The middle chapters help you identify which PMS triggers are contributing to your symptoms, and there are plenty of suggestions to help you overcome these triggers and move towards a better state of health.

Good nutrition is the cornerstone to a life with healthy and happy hormones, so getting your diet right is of great importance if you want to be free from PMS. Chapters 6 and 7 are all about diet, and help you understand that eating the wrong foods can make your PMS worse and eating the right foods can make your PMS better. Simply following the principles of a GI diet can help to switch off those monthly mood swings and sugar cravings, eating less salt can reduce premenstrual bloating and quitting caffeine can turn down anxiety. Yes, it's that simple!

There are plenty of natural remedies that I've seen work time and time again in my clinic. GLA helps with breast pain, chromium with sugar cravings and 5-HTP helps with premenstrual depression. Then there are hormone-balancing herbs like Agnus castus and effective plant extracts like phytoestrogens, DIM and indole-3-carbinol. Not to mention hormone-regulating nutrients such as the minerals magnesium and zinc and vitamins E and B6.

It's not just diet, exercise, supplements and lifestyle changes that can make a difference to PMS. There are a whole heap of natural therapies that can also help your body regain hormone balance. Acupuncture, homeopathy, aromatherapy massage and flower essences are to name but a few. These therapies all work in their own unique way, restoring hormone homeostasis. They can help coax a depleted body back into balance, calm an overstimulated nervous system, rejuvenate a weakened immune system and nourish a taxed hormonal system. Natural therapies, when used appropriately, restore, revive and revitalise the body, naturally allowing hormones to settle back into a state of balance.

What I've learnt about PMS from my own experience and from helping women in my clinic, is that every woman is different. There's no 'one size fits all' approach, each woman has her own unique set of symptoms and triggers, and has her own 'best' combination of supplements and therapies that will allow her hormones to come back into balance. What worked for me was a low alcohol, low cheese, low sugar diet accompanied by regular acupuncture. I also take a special form of natural or 'body identical' progesterone prescribed by a private doctor. You'll hear all about this kind of natural hormone therapy in chapter 8.

The chapters in this book are designed to help you go through a journey of self-discovery where you'll get to know what's causing your PMS and be able to make the best decision as to what to change in order to reduce your symptoms. You don't have to live with PMS and your family, your friends and your work colleagues don't have to live with your PMS either! This book can help guide you through.

Acknowledgements

With heartfelt thanks to . . .

Mum, Dad and Chris for 40+ years of unwavering support.

My husband Dax and our lovely boy Sonny, who make my life joyful and adventurous. Thanks for giving me the peace and quiet to make this book happen!

Sista Nem who is bold, brave and brilliant, Sezzie who is so wonderfully open-hearted and to my sister-in-law Claudine for her valued support and for rustling up the delicious recipes.

And Lauren for her guidance and wisdom and for keeping me on track!

Chapter One

What is PMS?

It's astonishing how many women across the world live with PMS (premenstrual syndrome). Gather any group of women together and you'll be amazed at the range of symptoms they experience each month and even more amazed at how it's generally accepted that PMS is 'expected' and simply 'lived with'. There's a generally accepted view that PMS is normal, just part of being a woman.

PMS doesn't just affect women, it also affects the people that these women live with, work with and socialise with. Parents, husbands and partners, children, friends and work colleagues have all developed coping strategies for this challenging time of month – presenting kind words, chocolates and support, or simply knowing that it's best to keep quiet and stay out of the way. And everyone breathes a sigh of relief as normality is once again restored.

So how did millions of women end up with PMS? It seems to me that from an early age, when you first develop symptoms and turn to your wiser elders for advice, the words of wisdom you hear are, 'Oh yes, I get that too, so does your sister and your granny – it's just your time of the month, it's PMS.'

Perhaps the message needs to change. If the responsive advice changes to, 'Ah those are signs that your hormones are out of balance but if you change your diet and lifestyle, take more exercise and reduce your stress then you'll soon be symptom free each month,' then PMS could become a thing of the past.

'PMS doesn't just affect women, it also affects the people that these women live with, work with and socialise with.'

Defining PMS

PMS has been troubling women for generations and those of us who suffer experience a group of symptoms normally 7-10 days before our period. These symptoms miraculously disappear as our period begins and return each month. The type of symptoms we experience and the intensity of these symptoms can vary from one month to another.

According to the NHS, nearly all women of childbearing age experience some premenstrual symptoms, but women between the ages of 20 and 40 are most likely to experience PMS. There are over 100 symptoms associated with PMS and you can read all about these symptoms in chapter 3.

'According to the NHS, nearly all women of childbearing age experience some premenstrual symptoms, but women between the ages of 20 and 40 are most likely to experience PMS.'

Types of PMS symptoms

- Emotional (psychological and behavioural).
- Physical.

Symptom check

What's clear is that PMS isn't the same for everyone. Some women experience PMS as just one or two mild symptoms and they see these symptoms as a warning sign that their period is on its way.

Other women experience symptoms that are so severe they seriously impact on their quality of life, forcing them to take time off work and impairing their relationships with their partners, family and friends. For these women PMS is much more debilitating.

What all PMS sufferers need to know is that it's possible to correct the hormone imbalance that triggers monthly symptoms. This book helps point you in the right direction, giving you the tools to know what to change and how to put those changes into practice to find relief from your PMS.

The history of PMS

PMS has been around since ancient times but it didn't receive any proper medical recognition until the early 60s. Different premenstrual symptoms were noted in medical journals from as early as the 30s through to the late 80s. Different countries around the world have different emphasis and opinions about PMS, with the Western world mainly accepting it as a recognisable sign that a woman is in her fertile years of her life, where her body undergoes hormonal changes that occur on a monthly cycle, triggering changes in mood and vitality.

Meet Dr Abraham

A cluster of premenstrual symptoms were first recorded in 1931, but it wasn't until the early 1980s that Professor Guy Abraham sorted the collection of symptoms into four different profiles. Now, more than three decades later, there are over 100 symptoms associated with PMS. The severity and number of symptoms that you can suffer from is incredibly variable and it's typical to experience symptoms from more than one of the four profiles that Abraham created.

These profiles have specific hormone imbalances and because of this they have very different approaches for symptom management. If you know your PMS profile then you can follow the diet and supplement advice for that profile which can help you find quick relief from your symptoms. Later on, in chapter 4, you'll discover how to work out your PMS profile.

'If you know your PMS profile then you can follow the diet and supplement advice for that profile which can help you find quick relief from your symptoms.'

PMS profiles

- PMS-A for anxiety.
- PMS-H for hydration (bloating).
- PMS-D for depression.
- PMS-C for cravings.

The good news

It's easy to get overwhelmed and bogged down by your symptoms each month. The good news is that there are plenty of options for you to explore, many of which have proven to be successful for many women who suffer from the same symptoms that you do. PMS is now considered to be a multifactorial condition that has its roots entangled in hormone imbalance created by poor diet, nutrient deficiencies, lack of exercise, stress and the depleting impact of an over-zealous lifestyle.

Medical approach

'If you do suffer from severe PMS then it's important that you visit your GP so that you can get other conditions ruled out.'

If you do suffer from severe PMS then it's important that you visit your GP so that you can get other conditions ruled out. The symptoms of PMS can be a warning sign for other conditions (endometriosis, polycystic ovary syndrome and pelvic inflammatory disorder) which will require a different type of treatment, so it's a good idea to get examined.

The medical approach to PMS is to encourage the use of self-help tools such as those discussed in this book – namely eating a healthy balanced diet, reducing salt, alcohol, sugar and saturated fat whilst increasing exercise and reducing stress. Some doctors do also encourage the use of supplements like evening primrose oil, vitamin B6 and zinc but many doctors will simply suggest the contraceptive pill. There are different types and strengths of the contraceptive pill and your GP will be able to match a suitable type to your range of symptoms. The hormones in the contraceptive pill can help to regulate hormone balance which helps to lift symptoms, easing PMS. However, there are pros and cons associated with the pill.

Is the contraceptive pill safe?

Many women are wary of taking the contraceptive pill because the synthetic hormones contained in the pill have been linked to an increased risk in developing female hormone-related cancers later on in life. Studies have shown that taking the pill increases your risk of developing breast cancer, endometrial cancer and ovarian cancer. These synthetic hormones are a similar shape to the hormones that your body produces so they have the same action as your own hormones but they have a much more powerful effect on body cells and this is what causes the problem.

Medical approaches to PMS

- The combined contraceptive pill.

- Progesterone only pill.

- A diuretic medication.

- Selective serotonin reuptake inhibitors (SSRIs).

- Gonadorelin analogue.

- Hysterectomy (only in severe cases and as a last resort).

Natural hormones

Some private doctors prefer to prescribe natural or 'body identical' hormones which have the same shape as the hormones that your body naturally produces. These have a much milder action on body cells compared to the synthetic hormones found in the contraceptive pill, which means they are much safer to take. According to experts, these hormones are equally effective at balancing hormones and relieving the symptoms of PMS. In chapter 8 you'll find out how to get in touch with a doctor that prescribes natural hormones.

Know your cycle

If you really want to start managing your symptoms then you are going to have to start taking notes about what happens to you across your cycle. You need to know your cycle length so you can start to predict when your premenstrual phase will occur. You're also going to have to get to know your symptoms – which symptoms do you have each month, which ones come and go and how severe are all of these symptoms?

Charting your symptoms

It's easy to forget how bad your PMS was last month when you've had 2-3 weeks of feeling great in-between. Charting your symptoms is the best way to gather and record all this information. There are many ways to do this. You can write the information in your day-to-day diary, you can use a pre-printed cycle chart or you can even use a phone app! Try a few different methods and find the one that works best for you. There's more information about this and an example of a pre-printed Symptom Chart in chapter 3.

Know your triggers

You'll also need to start gaining an awareness of your triggers. Is your PMS worse if you have had a very stressful month at work? Maybe it's worse if you've had lots of nights out, drinking more alcohol or perhaps a trigger for you is lack of exercise. If one month you suffer from much worse PMS than usual then ask yourself – what has been different this month? This is how you will gain insight into your PMS triggers. Chapters 5 and 6 provide you with details of all the common PMS triggers to consider.

Your PMS puzzle

All this information (symptoms, symptom severity, triggers) starts to show you your unique PMS puzzle, all of the pieces slowly coming together. This information is vital and will empower you to feel in-control of your PMS and will help motivate you to make changes with the knowledge that the changes you make, will have the results you desire.

Action points

▓ Start to think differently about your PMS. Realise that you don't have to experience PMS from now all the way up to your menopause. Consciously make a decision that you want to change. You can manage your PMS – your PMS doesn't get to manage you!

- Book an appointment to see your GP, discuss your symptoms and get other female hormone and physical related conditions ruled out.

- Look into ways to chart your cycle length, symptoms, symptom severity and think about ways to record possible triggers. What would work best for you – prepared chart, personal diary or a phone app?

Summing Up

- Now you know you are not alone. There are literally millions of women out there whose worlds also drastically change for a few days out of every month. PMS is real! It's not to be accepted as part and parcel of being a woman.

- Your PMS occurs because your body is unable to adjust to constantly changing hormone levels each month.

- You don't have to live with PMS, you can work out your triggers and you can change your diet, lifestyle and stress levels so that your body can cope with these necessary hormone changes, and you can live your life – uninterrupted.

Chapter Two

Your 28-Day Cycle

Ok, so here comes the science! If you want to get a grasp of your PMS then it's a good idea to get an understanding of what your monthly cycle is all about. You see nature intended a woman to be fertile from the age of puberty all the way up to the menopause.

This fertility is achieved through a 28-day cycle which has a major event slap bang in the middle at day 14 – ovulation. This incredible cycle is synchronised by a collection of glands and orchestrated by a group of hormones which work together to set the scene each month for a possible pregnancy.

Unfortunately, we haven't evolved to accommodate all the stresses and strains of modern-day life. All sorts of factors can cause the glands and hormones that are in charge of the cycle to get knocked out of balance. The result is PMS and other cycle-related issues.

'If you want to get a grasp of your PMS then it's a good idea to get an understanding of what your monthly cycle is all about.'

The glands in control

There are three glands – the hypothalamus, pituitary and ovaries – that work together to oversee the timings of your menstrual cycle. These glands ensure that the correct amounts of the necessary hormones are produced each month.

The hypothalamus

You could consider your hypothalamus to be 'the boss at the top', as this is the gland that's in charge. It's big and powerful and has the final say over what happens and when it happens. Your hypothalamus produces gonadotropin-releasing hormones, (GnRH), which can start your cycle up or shut it down at the flick of a switch.

The pituitary

Your pituitary gland acts like a 'middle man' keeping the hypothalamus informed with a moment to moment update of the overall hormonal status, whilst overseeing jobs like egg maturation, ovulation and hormone production. Your pituitary produces two hormones follicle-stimulating hormone and luteinizing hormone, nicknamed FSH and LH.

The ovaries

Your ovaries are your busy 'work force'. These glands contain a stock pile of eggs, which need to be matured and released at ovulation. They also contain specialised cells that produce vast quantities of oestrogen and progesterone which regulate your cycle and prepare your womb lining for a possibility of pregnancy.

Additional glands

There are two other glands that are not directly involved with the general running of your cycle but which have the power to trigger PMS.

The adrenal glands

These glands are in charge of your reaction to stress. They respond to stress by producing two hormones, adrenalin and cortisol, which help your body generate an appropriate reaction to the stress that you are under. If levels of cortisol become too high for too long, then this can disrupt your cycle regularity and trigger symptoms of PMS.

The thyroid gland

Your thyroid gland produces thyroxin, the hormone that drives your metabolic rate giving you the energy you need each day to feel full of life. If this gland becomes depleted and thyroxin production drops too low, then this can also affect your cycle and make your PMS symptoms more pronounced. You'll find out how having an underactive thyroid can trigger PMS in chapter 5.

The five key glands

- Hypothalamus.
- Pituitary.
- Ovaries.
- Adrenals.
- Thyroid.

Glands involved in the Female Cycle

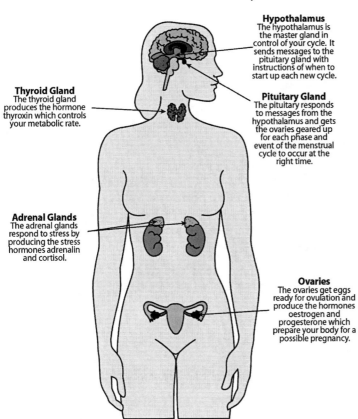

Hypothalamus
The hypothalamus is the master gland in control of your cycle. It sends messages to the pituitary gland with instructions of when to start up each new cycle.

Pituitary Gland
The pituitary responds to messages from the hypothalamus and gets the ovaries geared up for each phase and event of the menstrual cycle to occur at the right time.

Thyroid Gland
The thyroid gland produces the hormone thyroxin which controls your metabolic rate.

Adrenal Glands
The adrenal glands respond to stress by producing the stress hormones adrenalin and cortisol.

Ovaries
The ovaries get eggs ready for ovulation and produce the hormones oestrogen and progesterone which prepare your body for a possible pregnancy.

The hormone messengers

There are five main hormones that are involved in the smooth running of your menstrual cycle. These hormones act like messengers, bringing information and instructions to the glands about what should happen next. When in balance these hormones keep the cycle regular with ovulation occurring on day 14 and menstruation occurring on days 1-7.

Gonadotropin-releasing hormone – GnRH

GnRH is produced by your hypothalamus and is used to initiate two events of your menstrual cycle.

GnRH has two main jobs:

▨ Kick-starts the beginning of a new cycle.

▨ Sends a message that it's time for ovulation to happen.

Follicle-stimulating hormone – FSH

FSH is produced by your pituitary during the first 14 days of your menstrual cycle, which is called the follicular phase. FSH drives your cycle forward and it triggers around 10 to 200 eggs from the egg stores to start to mature. On day 14, the healthiest and biggest egg is selected for ovulation. This is just nature's way of helping you release your 'best' egg.

FSH also triggers oestrogen to be produced from special cells in your ovaries. Around day 12, oestrogen levels reach a massive peak, which means that FSH has completed its mission.

FSH has three main jobs:

▨ Helps get a new cycle started up.

▨ Tells the ovaries to ripen and mature eggs ready for ovulation.

▨ Instructs cells in the ovaries to produce lots of oestrogen.

Luteinizing hormone – LH

When FSH production stops on day 12, your pituitary switches to LH production. LH levels surge around day 14 and it's this surge that triggers ovulation. After ovulation LH triggers special cells in your ovaries to produce lots of progesterone and small amounts of oestrogen.

LH has three main jobs:

- To ensure ovulation takes place.
- Kick-starts progesterone production.
- To continue with oestrogen production.

Oestrogen

Oestrogen levels fluctuate across the cycle and this hormone has its highest activity during the earlier part of the cycle. At the beginning of each cycle oestrogen helps to prepare the womb in case the egg that's released at ovulation gets fertilised.

Oestrogen achieves this by getting cells in the womb lining to thicken creating a comfortable, cushioned area for your fertilised egg to nestle into.

Oestrogen has three main jobs:

- Prepares the womb for a possible fertilised egg.
- Helps to trigger ovulation to occur.
- Prepares breast tissue, ready for milk production.

Progesterone

This hormone is only produced after ovulation. Progesterone continues the good work that oestrogen started, thickening the womb lining and bringing in a rich blood supply to the womb lining, setting the scene for pregnancy.

Progesterone also increases your body temperature by half a degree, making sure that the womb is a warm environment, a perfect place for a fertilised egg to settle and develop.

Progesterone has three main jobs:

- Thickens the womb lining.
- Encourages a rich blood supply into the womb lining.
- Increases body temperature.

Eventually, around day 24, your body realises that fertilisation didn't happen. So your pituitary stops producing LH which in turn stops your ovaries producing progesterone and oestrogen. By day 28 both these hormones drop to an all-time low and your period begins.

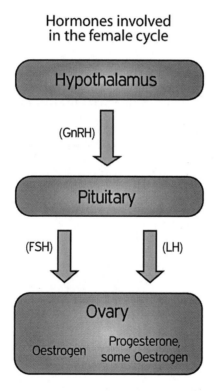

Hormones involved in the female cycle

20

Associated hormones

There are two other hormones that you need to become familiar with, these hormones aren't involved with the day-to-day running of the cycle but if they become out of balance they can throw your cycle out of sync and trigger PMS.

Testosterone

This hormone is generally linked to male fertility, but it's normal and healthy for women to produce small quantities of this hormone too. However some women can end up making too much testosterone and this can interfere with their cycle. A high level of testosterone has been linked with PMS-D (see chapter 4 for PMS profiles), especially for women who experienced anger, irritability, frustration, increased body hair and acne.

Prolactin

This hormone is normally produced during pregnancy when it helps to get breast tissue ready for milk production. However, some women have high levels of this hormone even when they aren't pregnant. Stress can cause prolactin levels to rise and this has been linked to premenstrual symptoms of breast tenderness and anxiety.

The seven key hormones

- Gonadotropin-releasing hormone (GnRH).
- Follicle stimulating hormone (FSH).
- Luteinizing hormone (LH).
- Oestrogen.
- Progesterone.
- Testosterone.
- Prolactin.

'Testosterone is generally linked to male fertility, but it's normal and healthy for women to produce small quantities of this hormone too.'

Hormone transport

The right balance of oestrogen and progesterone is essential for the smooth running of your cycle. These hormones are made in your ovaries but they need to travel around your body in order to keep your cycle in balance. They travel through your bloodstream, but they can't just dive into your bloodstream, they have to hitch a ride on special transport proteins which ferry them from place to place.

The two key transport proteins:

▦ Sex hormone-binding globulin (SHBG).

▦ Cortisol-binding globulin (CBG).

Sex hormone-binding globulin

'The right balance of oestrogen and progesterone is essential for the smooth running of your cycle.'

Sex hormone-binding globulin, nicknamed SHBG, is a transport protein that has the important job of ferrying oestrogen and testosterone around your body. SHBG is ultimately in control of oestrogen balance. If levels of SHBG are too low then not enough oestrogen gets ferried around your body, causing hormone imbalance.

Studies have shown that if you have high levels of SHBG then you'll be likely to suffer from PMS symptoms that relate to too much oestrogen, and if you have low SHBG then you're more likely to suffer from PMS symptoms that relate to high testosterone like acne and increased body hair.

Cortisol-binding globulin

Progesterone hitches a ride on the transport protein cortisol-binding globulin, better known as CBG. This protein carrier is also responsible for carrying the stress hormone cortisol. In fact, cortisol has a speedy boarding pass onto CBG, getting to go first while progesterone waits in line. This is why stress can be so disruptive to your hormone balance. The more stressed you are, the more cortisol you produce, making progesterone ineffective.

Cortisol-Binding Globulin ferries cortisol and progesterone around the body

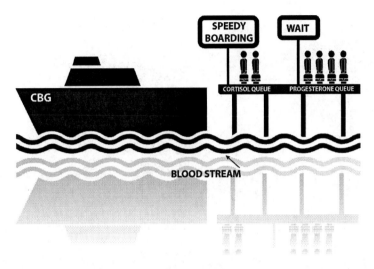

Synchronicity is the key

The magic of the female menstrual cycle is that all these glands, hormones and transport proteins work together to synchronise a 28-day cycle which has two phases (follicular phase and luteal phase) and two major events (ovulation and menstruation). PMS always and only occurs in the luteal phase of your cycle.

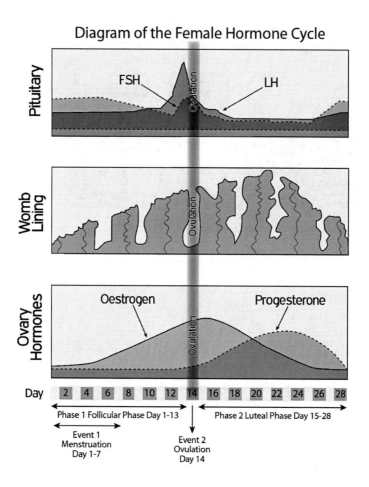

Diagram of the Female Hormone Cycle

Pituitary — FSH, Ovulation, LH

Womb Lining — Ovulation

Ovary Hormones — Oestrogen, Ovulation, Progesterone

Day: 2 4 6 8 10 12 14 16 18 20 22 24 26 28

Phase 1 Follicular Phase Day 1-13 | Phase 2 Luteal Phase Day 15-28

Event 1
Menstruation
Day 1-7

Event 2
Ovulation
Day 14

Event 1 – Menstruation (Your period)

The first day of your period marks the first day of a new 28-day cycle. During menstruation, the thick, nutritious womb lining generated during the last cycle literally falls away. This womb spring clean allows for a new lining to be built up, ensuring that if fertilisation takes place within this new cycle then the fertilised egg will have a fresh, clean and comfortable womb to develop in.

Need2Know

Phase 1 – The follicular phase

By day seven the follicular phase is well underway. During this phase eggs in the ovaries mature and a steady stream of oestrogen is produced. This oestrogen helps build a new thick womb lining. By day 12 oestrogen levels hit an all-time high and the most developed egg is selected for ovulation.

Event 2 – Ovulation

On day 14, the mature egg is released out into the fallopian tubes where it starts a six-day journey down into the womb. The egg leaves, carrying a bag of genetic material called chromosomes containing information and instructions on how to make a baby.

Phase 2 – Luteal phase

Cells in the ovaries produce large amounts of progesterone and small amounts of oestrogen. This progesterone quickly finishes off preparation work in the womb, thickening up the lining, bringing in a rich blood supply and increasing body temperature, ready for the arrival of the fertilised egg.

Around day 24, oestrogen and progesterone levels start to fall reaching a low enough level on day 28 to cause the womb lining to fall away.

This completes the end of another 28 day cycle and the start of the first day of another period and so your cycle continues to go on, and on, and on . . . until such a time that the egg stores are empty and menopause begins.

The cycle phases and events

- Menstruation: days 1-7
- Follicular phase: days 1-13.
- Ovulation: day 14.
- Luteal phase: days 15-28.

Communication is essential

Now you have a good understanding about the different phases of your menstrual cycle and you are aware of all the glands and hormones that need to be 'in-synch' for a regular 28-day cycle to be achieved. You can also now appreciate that your body needs certain factors to be in place, in order for all of the events within the 28-day cycle to fall into place.

Firstly the glands themselves need to be in good health, not too tired or preoccupied with other body chores. All of these glands need the right combination of nutrients to ensure good function and this is dependent on your diet and lifestyle.

Communication between the glands and hormones is essential and this is achieved by having enough of the transport proteins to ferry hormones through the bloodstream. Drinking too much alcohol, eating too much sugar and saturated fat and not taking enough exercise can lead to low levels of SHBG and CBG.

So what you eat and your level of activity influences the level and speed of communication between the glands and hormones involved in your cycle.

Factors that affect hormone transport:

- Poor liver function.
- High saturated fat diet.
- High alcohol intake.
- High sugar intake.
- Lack of exercise.
- High stress.

Restoring balance

If your cycle has become out of synch and if you are suffering from PMS then focusing on providing the glands with the nutrients they need to function properly and providing the right environment for the transport proteins to be at their best levels to ferry hormones around is of great importance. There are also lots of natural therapies that can help to recharge and restore your cycle back into a state of balance, and the benefits of these will be discussed in chapter 8.

Supportive nutrients

To fast-track out of PMS there are a few key nutrients that can quickly help you regain hormone balance and regulate transport protein activity. You'll be finding out more about these key nutrients and how they can help alleviate PMS in chapter 7.

The eight key nutrients:

- Magnesium.
- Zinc.
- Vitamin B6.
- Vitamin E.
- GLA.
- Omega-3.
- Phytoestrogens.
- Indoles.

Summing Up

■ This chapter might seem like a big biology lesson, but getting familiar with the names of the glands, hormones and transport proteins involved in your menstrual cycle will come in handy if you want to talk to your doctor or specialist about your PMS.

■ It's good to become familiar with the kind of words that your specialist might use when talking about your PMS. This way you can engage with the conversation instead of feeling blinded by science.

■ Remember, PMS is simply your body's way of letting you know that your hormones are out of balance.

Chapter Three

PMS Symptoms

Typical symptoms of PMS include decreased energy, tension, irritability, depression, headache, altered sex drive, breast pain, backache, abdominal pain, bloating and water retention. And remember, this is just a snapshot of the most commonly experienced symptoms from the list of over 100 possible PMS symptoms!

Although PMS affects 30-40% of women, it's thought that 80% of these women have learnt to 'cope' with their symptoms so they can continue with their day-to-day life. However, 5% of women experience emotional and physical symptoms to such a degree that it's impossible for them to continue with daily life. For these women their quality of life is severely disrupted.

What causes my symptoms?

The levels of hormones circulating around your body changes drastically throughout your 28-day cycle – there are massive highs mid-cycle and incredible lows just before and during your period.

At first it was thought that these changing levels of hormones alone caused symptoms of PMS. But now experts are viewing PMS slightly differently. They now think that the changing hormone levels across the cycle cause changes in the way the brain produces and reacts to neurotransmitters (brain chemicals that create your feelings, emotions, reactions and pain).

Science is producing the evidence to compound this belief and is revealing that women react differently to their brain chemicals during their premenstrual (luteal) phase of their cycle. It's this change in reaction to brain chemicals that allows the emotional and physical symptoms of PMS to manifest.

'Although PMS affects 30-40% of women, it's thought that 80% of these women have learnt to 'cope' with their symptoms so they can continue with their day-to-day life.'

Although the exact mechanisms and reasons for this still remain a mystery, what's clear is that oestrogen and progesterone interact with brain chemistry making moods and emotions more pronounced and extreme.

The PMS zone

By medical definition PMS occurs within the two weeks before your period. The length of time that you'll suffer from PMS each month is completely unique to you and can vary from month to month.

If you already have many of your triggers under control then you might experience just a few mild symptoms a couple of days before your period. But it's pretty typical for most women (who haven't already made any attempts to address their PMS) to experience symptoms 7-10 days before their period.

For some women though, it's quite a different story. If you are very unlucky or have a very poor diet and lifestyle, then you could experience symptoms for two weeks before your period and these symptoms could be very extreme and very debilitating.

PMS myths

It's important to dispel a few possible PMS myths. The definition of PMS can sometimes get confused and may women refer to any symptoms that they experience during their menstrual cycle as symptoms of PMS. But PMS shouldn't be used as an umbrella term for any twitch or twinge that you think might be hormone related. For a symptom to be connected to PMS it can only exist within the 14 days leading up to your period.

Some women also describe the discomfort and lack of energy that they experience during their period as part of their PMS picture. Again, this is not the case. PMS symptoms clear and ease off as soon as your period starts. Symptoms of exhaustion or fatigue during your period may be a sign that you are suffering from anaemia and this is especially common if you suffer from very heavy periods. Your doctor can run a test to determine if you are anaemic and can prescribe iron supplements to rectify this.

PMS symptoms

There are a phenomenal number of symptoms associated with PMS and they have conveniently been categorised into two groups – emotional (psychological and behavioural) and physical. The types of symptoms you can experience can vary from one month to the next but generally most women have a handful of core symptoms that they always experience.

Emotional symptoms

- Anxiety.
- Mood swings.
- Tiredness.
- Irritability.
- A drop in confidence.
- Clumsiness.
- Feeling upset or emotional.
- Feeling angry.
- Depressed mood.
- Crying and tearfulness.
- Difficulty concentrating.
- Confusion and forgetfulness.
- Restlessness.
- Decreased self-esteem.
- Loss of interest in sex.

'The types of symptoms you can experience can vary from one month to the next but generally most women have a handful of core symptoms that they always experience.'

Physical symptoms

- Headaches or migraine.
- Feeling bloated.
- Change in appetite.
- Abdominal (tummy) pain.
- Fluid retention.
- Changes to your skin and hair.
- Backache.
- Muscle and joint pain.
- Breast tenderness.
- Insomnia.
- Dizziness.
- Tiredness.
- Nausea.
- Weight gain (up to 1kg).
- Change in bowel habits.
- Food cravings.

PMS Symptom Questionnaire

Complete the following check list to discover your core and associated PMS symptoms which you can then assess each month.

Your core PMS symptoms

Tick the boxes for symptoms you experience every month. There are some blank boxes for you to fill in if you suffer from symptoms not listed.

☐ abdominal pain ☐ dizziness ☐ migraine

☐ anxiety ☐ fatigue ☐ mood swings

☐ backache ☐ feeling angry ☐ muscle aches

☐ bloating ☐ feeling upset ☐ nausea

☐ breast swelling ☐ fluid retention ☐ over- emotional

☐ breast tenderness ☐ forgetfulness ☐ poor concentration

☐ change in appetite ☐ headaches ☐ restlessness

☐ clumsiness ☐ insomnia ☐ salt cravings

☐ confusion ☐ irritability ☐ sugar cravings

☐ constipation ☐ joint pain ☐ tearfulness

☐ crying spells ☐ lack of confidence ☐ tiredness

☐ depressed mood ☐ low libido ☐ weight gain

☐ diarrhoea ☐ low self-esteem ☐ _____

Your associated PMS symptoms – Tick the boxes for symptoms you experience on an intermittent basis.

☐ abdominal pain ☐ dizziness ☐ migraine

☐ anxiety ☐ fatigue ☐ mood swings

☐ backache ☐ feeling angry ☐ muscle aches

☐ bloating ☐ feeling upset ☐ nausea

☐ breast swelling ☐ fluid retention ☐ over- emotional

☐ breast tenderness ☐ forgetfulness ☐ poor concentration

☐ change in appetite ☐ headaches ☐ restlessness

☐ clumsiness ☐ insomnia ☐ salt cravings

☐ confusion ☐ irritability ☐ sugar cravings

☐ constipation ☐ joint pain ☐ tearfulness

☐ crying spells ☐ lack of confidence ☐ tiredness

☐ depressed mood ☐ low libido ☐ weight gain

☐ diarrhoea ☐ low self-esteem ☐ _____

Charting your symptoms

Once you have completed the PMS Symptom Questionnaire and have identified your core and associated PMS symptoms you can transfer these onto your Monthly PMS Symptom Chart (see following pages) so that you can assess and track how your symptoms are changing each month. During each premenstrual phase you give your symptoms a score from 1-10, with 10 meaning that your symptoms are very pronounced and a score of 1 meaning that your symptoms are very mild. Scoring and tracking your symptoms in this way throughout the months that you are making changes to your diet and lifestyle enables you to keep track of the progress you are making. If you prefer you can use an online chart, a phone app or you can simply keep track of all your symptom/symptoms' scores in your diary or you can download and print out a chart from the Internet.

'PMS is a completely individual condition, your symptoms and symptom severity can change as your life changes or your PMS might stay the same each month for decades.'

PMS though the decades

PMS is a completely individual condition, your symptoms and symptom severity can change as your life changes, or your PMS might stay the same each month for decades. You might have times in your life when you are free from PMS and you might also have times when it's worse than ever before.

From over 15 years of working as a Nutritional Therapist helping women with all kinds of health issues, I've noticed that there are several times in a woman's life when she is more susceptible to PMS.

Your PMS may be worse:

▓ When you first start your periods.

▓ During your early twenties.

▓ When coming off the pill.

▓ After having a baby.

▓ Leading up to menopause.

Monthly PMS Symptom Chart

Month One

◾ 1. Transfer you core and associated symptoms onto this chart so you can assess your symptoms each month

◾ 2. Note down the date of the first day of your last period......

◾ 3. Count 15 days forward from the date of your last period and this will give you the date of day 15 of your cycle. Day 15-28 of your cycle is your PMS zone when you are likely to experience symptoms.

◾ 4. Every day between days 15 and 28 score your symptoms from 1-10, with 1 being mild and 10 being extreme.

◾ 5. Complete this chart for 1-6 months or until such a time that you feel you have your PMS symptoms under control.

Your PMS symptoms	Day of cycle													
	15	16	17	18	19	20	21	22	23	24	25	26	27	28

Month Two

Your PMS symptoms	Day of cycle													
	15	16	17	18	19	20	21	22	23	24	25	26	27	28

Month Three

Your PMS symptoms	Day of cycle													
	15	16	17	18	19	20	21	22	23	24	25	26	27	28

Teenage PMS

The transition from girl to woman isn't always a smooth one. It can take a while for the glands to work out how much of each hormone they are supposed to produce, and the communication system between glands and hormones can be a little unreliable to start with. Consequently, the lead up to your very first period can be rather a bumpy one. This is a troubling and emotional time. Your body shape is undergoing some rather radical changes and your emotions appear to be super-charged – and this is your introduction to life with 'fluctuating' hormones!

This rocky road can continue throughout the first few cycles and the pressure of teenage life certainly doesn't work in favour of helping these hormones acclimatise. Exposure at such a young age to media trends channelled through TV shows, fashion magazines, websites and blogs means that young women put themselves under extreme pressure to be 'body beautiful', often aspiring to be like their favourite celebrity. The stress generated from this and other peer-related activities and fad dieting can send a young woman's cycle into a spin, delivering a highly-charged PMS phase of life.

Making changes

- Follow a healthy (not extreme) exercise regime – this helps ease teenage anxieties and helps get hormones in balance.

- Ditch fad dieting and stick to a healthy eating plan that focuses on fish, chicken, turkey, lots of vegetables and wholegrains and snack on fresh fruits.

- Hydrate your body with 1-2 litres of water a day – this will help your skin and your hormones improve.

- Find ways to smooth over your insecurities and choose to be around friends that are supportive and understanding. The more settled you feel the more settled your hormones will be.

- Don't believe everything you read in a magazine, follow your instincts and 'do' what feels right for you.

- Realise your potential – you are young and you have a great future ahead of you, so relax and take your time.

- If your PMS becomes really unbearable then think twice before taking the contraceptive pill, try some natural alternatives first.

- Supplement with vitamin B6 and zinc to help regulate your cycle and balance hormones.

Leaving home PMS

During the years when you lived at home you were hopefully very fortunate to live in a loving, safe and nourishing environment. It's likely that you were sheltered from exposure to financial worries and generally lived life with minimum stress, plenty of sleep and had access to a fridge full of food and home-cooked meals.

It's not unusual for young adults to 'go wild' when they first leave home. A few years of college or university or sharing a house with friends can, for some, mean a downturn in health, and it's your hormones that end up taking a hit. Student diets are generally nutritionally poor – full of refined carbohydrates, fried foods and saturated fat with limited fresh vegetables and fruit. (For healthy student advice and recipes see *Student Cookbook – A Healthy Eating Guide*, Need2Know.)There are plenty of late nights and a sharp incline in alcohol consumption which are all a factors for PMS. After college or university, stress levels are notched up a gear with exposure to financial responsibilities and the added stress that the workplace brings. Increased intake of caffeine can also accentuate symptoms of PMS.

Making changes

- If your lifestyle has become very toxic then supplement with milk thistle a herb that aids liver function.

- Find healthy ways to socialise – team sports can be of great benefit.

- Top up your freezer with frozen green vegetables and edamame beans, they are as nutritious as fresh vegetables, but they last a lot longer.

- The more tired and wired you are the more your hormones will suffer, so get a few early nights so your body can recharge.

- Limit tea or coffee to one cup a day – caffeine can play havoc with your hormones.

Post-pill PMS

There are undoubtedly times in a woman's life when contraception is necessary. This is of course personal choice, but for generations the contraceptive pill has been one of the most convenient methods of contraception. However, as scientific evidence emerges drawing attention to the fact that taking the contraceptive pill enhances your risk of developing certain cancers and heart disease, more and more women are shying away from this method of contraception.

It's not unusual for young adults to be prescribed the pill at an early age to help regulate the cycle, dampen down heavy bleeding or curb extremely painful periods. Women can end up staying on the contraceptive pill for five, 10 or even 15 years. It's not until they think about starting a family – which could be in their 30s, that the contraceptive pill gets put to one side.

Whilst you've been taking the contraceptive pill the finely tuned system that normally regulates your cycle (glands and hormones) has been taking a bit of a snooze. In some cases it's very hard to awaken the glands and kick-start your natural cycle back into action. Cycle absence and irregularity is very common, and symptoms of PMS can occur either randomly or for long periods of time as your cycle re-boots itself.

Your cycle should eventually become established but your PMS may be worse than ever before. Some experts believe this may be a result of synthetic hormones from the contraceptive pill lingering in your system.

Making changes

- Consider homeopathy – this is a great way to detox the contraceptive pill.

- Consider acupuncture – this is very effective for improving communication between glands and hormones, creating balance and reducing PMS.

- Eat more broccoli – this and other cruciferous vegetables contain a substance that helps your body eliminate oestrogen.

Post-pregnancy PMS

It's not unusual for me to hear a woman say, 'I didn't really suffer from PMS until after I'd had my children.' Well during pregnancy your body experiences levels of oestrogen, progesterone and prolactin that are far greater than it's ever experienced before. Before pregnancy the glands that control your cycle responded to specific thresholds or concentration of these hormones to keep your cycle regular and your symptoms of PMS under control.

During pregnancy these glands experience levels of hormones that far exceed the normal thresholds and this can cause the glands to be less sensitive to the normal thresholds once the pregnancy is over. This can leave your hormones out of balance. With the extreme lack of sleep and the fact that your body could be nutritionally depleted from the pregnancy and breastfeeding, it's no surprise that you've got PMS.

Making changes

- Catch up on sleep – this will help your body recover from the pregnancy and will help your hormones come back into balance.
- Eat a highly nutritious diet – tempting as it is to live off toast and baby snacks because you're too tired to cook, your body needs good nutrition to recover.
- Increase oily fish – the omega-3 oils that they contain are very important for cell receptor sites and this means your glands can start being more sensitive to your hormones again.
- Up your exercise – having a new baby can be exhausting but finding the time to fit cardiovascular exercise into you week helps to boost levels of the transport proteins which improves hormone balance.

Need2Know

Peri-menopause PMS

Most women start to wind down their fertility around the age of 50, but everyone is different. A rule of thumb is that you are likely to experience a similar fertility lifespan as your mother. In the years leading up to the menopause your periods can start to change. Some women find their periods become very light and scanty whilst others have an opposite experience.

As you travel through your peri-menopause your oestrogen and progesterone levels start to decline. Women with low progesterone can experience PMS with extreme fatigue and unbearable headaches, they can feel depleted and their mood can be unusually low.

Making changes

- Consider a course of acupuncture or reflexology to help your hormones wind down smoothly.

- Ask your doctor to run some hormone tests to assess if you are heading towards the menopause.

- Supplement with the herb Agnus castus which helps to boost progesterone levels.

- Talk to your doctor about using a natural progesterone cream or capsule as this can be very effective. Alternatively, find a private doctor if your own doctor doesn't deal with natural progesterone, as many doctors don't.

- Sign up for some yoga classes – these help to keep your body toned and your nervous system relaxed.

Action plan

- Time to take note of your symptoms! Complete the Symptom Questionnaire this month to discover your core PMS symptoms. You can then transfer these symptoms onto your Monthly PMS Symptom Chart, so you can keep note of how severe your symptoms are each month. This is a great way to track your progress.

- Consider when your PMS started or think about times when your PMS has been particularly bad, make a note of when these were. If this matches any of the PMS situations mentioned then start to follow the 'Making changes' advice.

Summing Up

▪ There are a number of symptoms that you can experience if you have PMS, and the main ones fall into one of two categories – emotional or physical.

▪ Your symptoms can vary from month to month but there are probably a core collection of specific symptoms that stay with you month after month.

▪ There are likely to be times in your life when your PMS is a lot worse, but there are plenty of natural approaches and solutions to help you through these times.

Chapter Four

PMS Profiles

So far you will have grasped an understanding of how your menstrual cycle works. You've taken a note of how long your cycle is, what your main symptoms are, determined how severe each of your symptoms are and you've reflected back through your life and taken note of when your worst episodes of PMS occurred.

It's now time to work out what your PMS profile is. Why do you need this information? Well, because your PMS profile gives you clues about the type of hormone imbalance driving your PMS forward. By discovering which hormones are out of balance you can be very specific about the type of healing path you choose, which is handy if you want to sort out your PMS in a hurry.

Dr Abraham, the pioneer of PMS

Back in 1983, Dr Abraham published a scientific paper in the *Journal of Reproductive Medicine* where he revealed to the world his new classification system for PMS. Dr Abraham's system was based on his findings that women with the same 'type' of symptoms shared the same 'type' of hormone imbalance. Dr Abraham was a true PMS pioneer as his new classification system became an established model which helped doctors all over the world develop a deeper understand of PMS – how to approach and treat this condition.

It's all in your mind!

PMS isn't just down to the hormone imbalances that Dr Abraham devised. It's now known that these hormone patterns cause an imbalance in brain chemicals and that's why women end up 'feeling' and experiencing their PMS symptoms. So before we get started on the different PMS profiles it's worth getting a quick overview of the different brain chemicals (neurotransmitters) that are involved in PMS. These include adrenalin, noradrenalin, dopamine and serotonin and here's how these brain chemicals make you feel . . .

Chemical reactions

- Adrenalin – anxiety.

- Noradrenalin – hostility, irritability.

- Normal serotonin levels – happy, relaxed.

- Low serotonin – depressed.

- High serotonin – nervous tension, palpitations, water retention, poor concentration.

- Dopamine – relaxed, mentally focused.

Four PMS profiles

The four classifications or profiles that Dr Abraham created are: PMS-A, PMS-H, PMS-D and PMS-C. Although the symptoms and hormone patterns experienced within each profile are very clearly defined, the reality is that it might not initially be clear which profile you belong to.

To start with you may have so many varied symptoms that your PMS may appear to fit into more than one profile. This is very normal and as you start to make changes to your diet and lifestyle many of your symptoms will quickly ease away, leaving a few core symptoms that are more likely to be from just one PMS profile.

PMS-A for anxiety

This profile is extremely common, with around 80% of PMS sufferers experiencing this profile. Symptoms associated with this profile include anxiety, tension, irritability, mood swings and nervous tension. So what about hormones and brain chemicals? Well, women with PMS-A typically have too much oestrogen or a high oestrogen to progesterone ratio. Women with this PMS profile have high levels of, and are very sensitive to, adrenalin, noradrenalin and serotonin, whilst having too little dopamine. It's this hormone and brain chemical pattern that causes these women to feel more anxious, tense and 'on edge'.

Finding ways to lower excess oestrogen can be of great help. Eating foods rich in phytoestrogens helps to dampen down oestrogen activity and increasing foods that boost liver function are also of benefit.

PMS-A at a glance

- Symptoms – anxiety, tension, irritability, mood swings, nervous tension.

- Hormone imbalance – too much oestrogen or a high oestrogen to progesterone ratio.

- Neurotransmitter pattern – too much adrenalin, noradrenalin and serotonin and too little dopamine.

PMS-C for cravings

As this title suggests, this PMS profile is all about appetite. Women in this profile have an increased desire to eat carbohydrates – sweets, chocolates, pastries, cakes, biscuits, toast, bread and pasta – basically anything sweet or starchy! Other symptoms include headaches, fatigue, fainting spells and palpitations which are all related to blood sugar imbalance.

PMS has long had the reputation of being associated with chocolate and that's because around 40% of women with PMS experience the PMS-C profile. So how do these uncontrollable cravings come about?

Studies have shown that women with PMS-C produce much higher amounts of insulin during the 5-10 days before their period, compared to other times in their cycle. Insulin is the hormone that your body uses to get sugar out of your bloodstream and into body cells. These high levels of insulin pull too much sugar out of your bloodstream causing extreme blood sugar lows. In an attempt to fix this blood sugar low, your brain creates cravings for sugary and starchy foods. No wonder chocolate seems like such a good idea! Experts believe that this extra dollop of insulin may occur due to a magnesium deficiency.

Dietary changes are particularly powerful for this PMS profile. Following a diet that helps to keep blood sugar levels balanced can be of great benefit. Eating plenty of low GI and GL foods and supplementing with magnesium and chromium can help to stabilise insulin levels and ease cravings.

PMS-C at a glance

- Symptoms – increase in appetite, sugar or starchy food cravings, headaches, energy dips, fatigue, palpitations, fainting, the 'shakes'.

- Hormone imbalance – too much insulin.

- Nutrients – magnesium deficiency.

PMS-H for hydration

This is a very popular profile with an estimated 66% of sufferers experiencing PMS-H. During the lead up to your period you might notice that your clothes are feeling a little tighter than normal and if you suffer from PMS-H then this is definitely something that you'll identify with. To officially fit into this profile you'll need to gain more than three pounds (1.4kg) before your period. Don't worry, this weight gain occurs due to water retention and as your hormones change after your period, you'll shed the weight again. You are likely to feel very bloated and your hands, feet, ankles and face could become puffy. Abdominal pain and breast tenderness is also on the menu for this PMS profile.

Why so huffy and puffy? Well women in this profile tend to have too much of a hormone called aldosterone during the premenstrual phase of their cycle. Aldosterone tells your body to hold on to water which is why you end up all puffed up. Too much stress and too much oestrogen stimulate your body to make too much aldosterone. Normally the brain chemical dopamine helps to calm aldosterone down, but it's been found that women with PMS-H have too little dopamine to get their water retention in check.

You won't go doing yourself any favours if you are sprinkling salt all over your food or tucking into salty snacks. The sodium in the salt makes aldosterone levels climb sky high, puffing you up like a bloated fish! Increasing foods rich in magnesium helps to counterbalance the effects of sodium and finding ways to reduce stress can help reduce your puffiness.

PMS-H at a glance

- Symptoms – water retention, swollen hands, face, feet and ankles, swollen abdomen, breast tenderness, weight gain.

- Hormone imbalance – too much oestrogen and too much aldosterone.

- Neurotransmitter pattern – too little dopamine.

PMS-D for depression

This is by far the least popular profile with just 27% of sufferers experiencing this group of symptoms. PMS-D is all about low mood, and by low mood I mean a change from your normal mood into a gloomy, confused, tearful, sleepless, desperate altered state of reality.

Women with PMS-D have been found to have low levels of oestrogen and high levels of progesterone during the luteal phase of their cycle. The drop in oestrogen is thought to send serotonin plummeting which is why your mood takes a nosedive. High levels of stress can also cause this group of women to have higher levels of testosterone which means you can become angry, confrontational and well – a bit hairy. And if you didn't already have enough to feel depressed about, then the added input of too much testosterone could also cause your skin to become oily and spotty. No wonder this is the least popular PMS profile!

PMS-D at a glance

- Symptoms – depression, low mood, crying, forgetfulness, confusion, insomnia, clumsiness, feeling withdrawn, lack of co-ordination.

- Hormone imbalance – too little oestrogen and too much progesterone and possibly too much testosterone.

* Neurotransmitter pattern – too little serotonin.

Premenstrual dysphoric disorder

Dr Abraham's classification system has stood the test of time but it became apparent as the years rolled on that an additional profile needed to be added. In the 1990s a new profile stemming from PMS-D was devised and classified as premenstrual dysphoric disorder (PMDD), now estimated to affect 5% of PMS sufferers. PMDD has the same hormone and neurotransmitter pattern as PMS-D but the symptoms are extremely pronounced and potentially dangerous. If you suffer from PMDD then you'll recognise that during the week leading up to your period you experience an altered sense of reality, your emotions are highly charged and you are unpredictable, inflammatory and unsettled. Some experts suggest that this group express the symptoms of obsessive personality disorders.

Symptoms of PMDD

* Suicidal thoughts.

* Extreme depression.

* Extreme emotional distress.

* Psychosocial impairment.

* Obsessive behaviour.

* Desire to harm self or others.

Appropriate treatment

I've come face-to-face with PMDD in my clinic. A lady came to see me with the goal of addressing her PMS. We talked through her diet and lifestyle which were surprisingly good. When we came to discussing her symptoms she fell apart. Her words have always stuck in my mind, she said, 'I become a different person before my period, I don't even recognise who I am, it's like my body has been taken over by someone else and all I can do is watch from the sideline as it all happens in front of me. I become filled with immense rage, anger and frustration. I get so wound up that eventually I just explode and I go at my husband and physically attack him.'

As much as I'm a firm believer in nutritional therapy and other complementary therapies, I also know that there are some conditions that do require intervention with conventional medicine – and PMDD is one of those conditions. Changing your diet and lifestyle, taking more exercise and finding ways to deal with stress does have a phenomenal impact on all of the other PMS profiles. However, the biochemical imbalances that exist for women in the PMDD group is not going to be shifted by taking a few yoga classes, swallowing a few herbs or vitamins and eating more vegetables.

If you think that you suffer from PMDD then waste no time in getting proper help and support. Your condition is 'real' and during your premenstrual phase you are at risk of hurting yourself and the people that you love and that love you. Book an appointment to see your doctor, express your concerns that you are suffering from PMDD and ask to be referred to a specialist. Don't settle for being fobbed off – explain your circumstances and your symptoms until you are taken seriously. Your doctor can prescribe an appropriate mood-stabilising medication to help you feel much more 'in control' of your emotions and your actions. You'll be able to feel like 'you' for the whole of the month, every month.

Action plan

- Time to work out your PMS profile. Complete the PMS Profile Questionnaire overleaf to work out which PMS profile is relevant to you.

- If you have so much as an inkling that you suffer from PMDD then book an appointment to see your GP and explore the medications, support, counselling or psychotherapy that are offered to you.

PMS Profile Questionnaire

Complete this questionnaire by reflecting back over your last pre-menstrual phase and score your symptoms accordingly using the scale below. Your PMS Profile is the profile that has your highest score.

Scoring your symptoms

0 = symptoms does not exist for you

1 = mild symptom

2 = moderate symptom

3 = sever symptom that interferes with your daily activities

4 = severe symptom which you are unable to cope with and prevents you from living your life normally

PMS – A

☐ anxiety

☐ Irritability

☐ mood swings

☐ nervous tension

☐ feeling 'on edge'

Total

PMS – H

☐ breast tenderness

☐ puffy face, feet or hands

☐ swollen abdomen

☐ water retention

☐ weight gain

Total

PMS – C

☐ energy dips and fatigue

☐ headaches

☐ increased appetite

☐ palpitations

☐ sugar and food cravings

Total

PMS – D

☐ clumsiness or poor co-ordination

☐ confusion or forgetfulness

☐ crying spells

☐ low mood or depression

☐ insomnia

Total

Adapted from Dr Guy Abraham's Menstrual Symptom Questionnaire first published in 1983 in the *Journal of Reproductive Medicine*.

Summing Up

- Remember it's very common to have symptoms in more than one profile and to be unsure as to which one is your main profile. For instance, both PMS-H and PMS-A are triggered by high oestrogen so it's very likely that you'll have symptoms for both of these profiles.

- Even though there are some very specific dietary and supplement advice for each PMS profile, the general dietary and lifestyle advice for PMS has a very positive impact on all PMS profiles.

Chapter Five

Hormone Imbalance

Although many of the physiological and biochemical causes linked to PMS are still baffling scientists, there are many contributory factors that have become well-known triggers for hormone imbalance. The main hormones that are involved with PMS are oestrogen, progesterone, testosterone and prolactin, and there are plenty of ways to help get these hormones back in balance.

Oestrogen and progesterone

Oestrogen and progesterone were designed to work in harmony with each other. Oestrogen is a very 'stimulating' hormone, it causes smooth muscles to contract, fires up your brain, allows better access to your memory, charges up your nervous system, plumps up your skin, tightens your artery and capillary walls and stimulates cells in your womb lining and breast to grow rapidly. All in all, oestrogen is a very 'active' hormone.

Progesterone has quite the opposite effect, having a more calming action on the body and it helps to keep oestrogen in check. Progesterone relaxes your mind and mood, it smoothes over frazzled nerves and eases muscular and cardiovascular tension.

'In the first half of your cycle oestrogen gets your body wound up and in the second half of your cycle progesterone calms everything down.'

So in the first half of your cycle oestrogen gets your body wound up and in the second half of your cycle progesterone calms everything down. If your hormone levels are out of synch and you end up producing too much oestrogen in the first half of your cycle then you won't have enough progesterone in the second half of your cycle (before your period) to calm yourself down. So you literally remain wound up during the premenstrual phase of your cycle.

Or if you don't produce enough oestrogen during the first half of your cycle and you produce too much progesterone in the second half of your cycle then you body is going to end up too suppressed and your mood will dip too low.

Cycle clues

▪ High oestrogen causes periods to become very heavy, lasting seven or more days with plenty of clots, cramps and period pain.

▪ Low oestrogen causes periods to become light, lasting just 3-5 days, with just one or two days of full flow.

Too much oestrogen

Our Western diet and lifestyle tends to make it very easy for a woman's oestrogen levels to climb too high. Stress can also cause your body to produce too much oestrogen, as can a diet high in red meat, dairy products (particularly cheese, ice cream and cream), caffeine, sugar and alcohol.

'Our Western diet and lifestyle tends to make it very easy for a woman's oestrogen levels to climb too high.'

Xenoestrogens

There are a group of environmental oestrogens called xenoestrogens found in our water supply and food chain. These synthetic oestrogens are far more powerful than the natural oestrogen that your body produces, which makes them very harmful and potentially dangerous. If you do have a high intake of xenoestrogens this will push up your oestrogen activity leaving you with oestrogen-associated symptoms of PMS each month.

Making changes

▪ Drink filtered water and avoid water in plastic bottles, as this helps reduce your exposure to xenoestrogens.

▪ Avoid buying food wrapped in plastic or using cling film in such a way that it has direct contact with your food. This will also help to reduce your xenoestrogen exposure.

▪ Cut back on red meat and dairy products to help reduce your oestrogen levels.

▪ Eat more broccoli and other cruciferous vegetables, as this helps your liver clear oestrogen from your body.

- Include phytoestrogens in your diet, as these help to normalise oestrogen levels. These include soya beans, tofu, tempeh, miso, fennel, alfalfa, lentils and flaxseeds.

- Supplement with vitamin B6 as high oestrogen levels cause vitamin B6 deficiency.

- If your GP or Nutritional Therapist has run some hormone tests and you have been diagnosed with high oestrogen levels then supplement with DIM, indole-3-carbinol or calcium D-glucarate to help correct this.

Too little oestrogen

If your pituitary is feeling exhausted from the effects of long-term stress then it may be unable to produce enough FSH to stimulate the ovaries to produce enough oestrogen. If you are very underweight or have suffered shock or trauma then this can also cause oestrogen levels to fall short, as can chronic fatigue, anorexia and exhaustion.

Making changes

- Supplement with zinc and vitamin B6, as these nutrients help the pituitary recover.

- Don't leave long times in-between meals and snacks. Your body needs small frequent healthy meals to recover.

- If stress is a factor then consider counselling or find ways to ease your schedule and settle relationships.

- Consider a course of acupuncture or reflexology to help give your ovaries and hormones a boost.

Testosterone

This hormone is mainly associated with men and many women don't realise that it's perfectly normal and healthy to produce a little testosterone each month. However being too stressed and drinking too much caffeine can cause your testosterone levels to become too high. Increased facial and body hair, oily skin, acne and feeling angry, frustrated and confrontational are all telltale signs that testosterone has climbed too high.

High levels of testosterone can be a risk factor for polycystic ovary syndrome better known as PCOS. So if you think your levels of testosterone are on the up then it's worth visiting your GP to get PCOS ruled out.

Making changes

- Find ways to reduce your stress and lighten your load.

- Cut out caffeine which includes tea, coffee, colas and energy drinks. Chocolate also contains small amounts of caffeine.

- Supplement with the herb saw palmetto as this helps get testosterone levels in check.

Prolactin

Prolactin is the hormone that women make during pregnancy and its job is to get the breast tissue ready for making breast milk once the baby arrives. Prolactin is very much linked to the calming neurotransmitter dopamine, which prevents prolactin levels from becoming too high. Prolactin becomes part of the PMS puzzle when you become too stressed as stress causes dopamine levels to drop which means that prolactin is free to do as it pleases. High prolactin levels contribute to water retention and breast pain and tenderness.

Having high levels of oestrogen also encourages your body to make more prolactin and high prolactin levels reduce your ability to produce progesterone. So if your prolactin levels are on the up, then your progesterone levels will be falling down. Not enough progesterone to counterbalance oestrogen means that symptoms associated with high oestrogen can also occur – the perfect conditions for PMS-A and PMS-H.

Making changes

* Dealing with stress should be a priority – exercise, yoga, counselling, massage and reflexology can all be of help.

* Reducing caffeine and eating a diet full of low GI foods is also of great benefit

* Supplementing with zinc, magnesium and liquorice helps to normalise prolactin and dopamine levels.

* Vitamin E has been found in studies to help relieve symptoms of breast tenderness.

Transport proteins

Your ability to produce the transport proteins which ferry hormones around your body affects your hormone balance and PMS. Research has revealed that being overweight, eating a diet high in saturated fat, drinking too much alcohol and taking too little cardiovascular exercise can prevent your liver from making enough of the transport proteins such as SHBG.

Making changes

* Start taking regular cardiovascular exercise.

* If you are overweight then follow a healthy eating plan to get your BMI into normal range.

* Include phytoestrogens from soya foods (soya yoghurt, miso, tempeh) and flaxseeds in your daily diet.

* Cut back on alcohol, sugar, caffeine and saturated fat (red meat and dairy products).

* Supplement with milk thistle which acts as a liver tonic.

'Research has revealed that being overweight, eating a diet high in saturated fat, drinking too much alcohol and taking too little cardiovascular exercise reduces your levels of transport proteins.'

Hormone testing

If you are finding all the science a bit heavy and have looked at your symptoms and PMS profile but remain confused as to what sort of hormone imbalance might be driving your PMS forward, then you could ask your doctor to run a blood test. This will give you a snapshot of your hormone pattern.

A more accurate way to test your hormone levels is to use a Female Hormone Panel which involves taking 11-13 saliva samples across the month, giving you a map of your oestrogen and progesterone levels across your cycle. A Nutritional Therapist can arrange this test for you or you can go direct to one of the testing clinics in the UK.

Making changes

- Visit www.bant.org.uk to search for a Nutritional Therapist in your area who you can organise a Female Hormone Panel.
- Go direct to Genova Testing Laboratory who have a clinic in London, visit www.gdx.net for more information.

Poor liver function

It's your liver that breaks down your hormones, processing and packaging them ready for removal from the body. If your liver is tired and sluggish or preoccupied with other functions, like detoxification or processing dietary fats, then it's unlikely to keep up with these hormone-clearing chores. Consequently, your hormones become out of balance and you start to experience PMS.

Making changes

- Clean up your act – cut back on alcohol, caffeine, social drugs, nicotine and processed foods, as all of these stress your liver's ability to detoxify.
- Cut back on saturated fat and fried food, as too much fat can clog up your liver.

- Increase celery, chicory, endive, garlic, leeks, turmeric and chilli, as these can help to improve liver function.
- Supplement with milk thistle, dandelion, artichoke, choline, inositol and B-vitamins, as these can help to refresh your liver and improve oestrogen clearance.

Constipation

Once your liver has packaged up your used hormones it passes these waste parcels into your intestine where they bind to fibre and are safely transported out of your body. This is a pretty smooth system if your bowels are working properly. However if you have constipation, don't eat enough fibre or don't have enough 'friendly' gut bacteria then your packaged parcels of waste hormones end up hanging around in your intestines rather than being excreted. This gives them the chance to be reabsorbed back into your body which puts a strain on your liver and causes oestrogen levels to climb, setting the scene for those oestrogen-related PMS symptoms to occur.

Making changes

- Increase fibre in your diet to get your bowels emptying at least once if not twice a day.
- Drink at least two litres of water a day, as this will also help to improve bowel function.
- If you have increased your fibre and water levels but are still bunged up then supplement with a natural laxative, keeping regular is very important.
- Take a probiotic, as this helps to freshen-up your intestine and improve oestrogen clearance.

BMI and body fat

Scientists have discovered that fat cells contain enzymes that can make oestrogen. So the more fat cells your body contains and the fuller these fat cells are, the more oestrogen your body makes. Your body mass index, also known as your BMI, will give you an indication of whether you are underweight, have normal weight, are overweight or suffer from obesity. If you are overweight or obese then you have a considerable amount of body fat which is churning out a constant stream of oestrogen. No wonder you have PMS, as all this extra oestrogen will be causing your hormones to be out of balance.

'Fat cells contain enzymes that can make oestrogen. So the more fat cells your body contains the more oestrogen your body makes.'

Calculate your BMI

It's very easy to calculate your BMI all you need is your weight and your height and you can cross reference these two measurements on the BMI Chart to see which BMI range your body falls within.

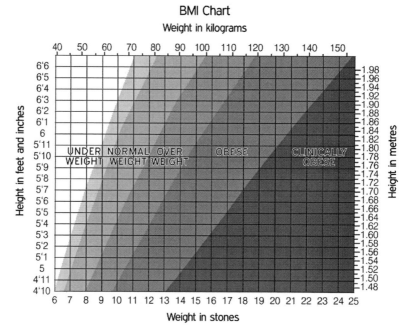

BMI Chart

Making changes

- If your BMI indicates you are overweight or obese, then it's time to shape up. Follow a healthy eating plan that is low in fat, sugar, salt and alcohol and high in lean protein, wholegrains, pulses, fruits and vegetables.

- Increase your cardiovascular exercise to burn off all that extra body fat. Joining a gym and getting an exercise plan designed for you by a personal trainer can help you stay motivated.

- Supplements with 'lipotopic' agents help your liver break down and eliminate excess fat from your body. These include methionine, inositol and choline.

- Supplementing with herbs like dandelion, artichoke and milk thistle as these help support your liver and gall bladder.

Underactive thyroid

There is a great deal of evidence that links an underactive thyroid with PMS and vice versa. Having an underactive thyroid is a very common disorder with 1-4% of the population experiencing moderate to severe hypothyroidism (the medical name for an underactive thyroid) and as many as 12% experiencing mild or 'sub-clinical' hypothyroidism, and your risk of developing this condition increases as you get older.

Having hypothyroidism means that your thyroid gland doesn't make enough of the hormone thyroxin which controls your metabolic rate (the speed at which all biological processes in your body take place). There are a number of factors that cause hypothyroidism, including ongoing stress, shock, trauma and selenium and iodine deficiency, and many women experience hypothyroidism after having a baby. Hypothyroidism is a sign that your body is tired and depleted. Your GP can do a simple blood test to determine whether you suffer from this condition.

'An underactive thyroid can be caused by ongoing stress, shock, trauma and selenium or iodine deficiency and many women experience hypothyroidism after having a baby.'

Symptoms of hypothyroidism:

- Low mood.
- Fatigue.
- Sensitivity to the cold.
- Cold hands and feet.
- Dry skin.
- Headaches.
- Weight gain.
- Difficulty losing weight.
- Recurrent infections.
- Menstrual problems.
- PMS.

Making changes

- Slow down, take time out, sleep and rest so your body can recover and shake off the stress response.
- Eating sea vegetables (seaweeds) which are rich in iodine can help to nourish a tired thyroid gland.
- Avoid eating uncooked turnips, cabbage, broccoli, Brussels sprouts, soya beans, peanuts, pine nuts and millet, as these contain goitrogens which stop your thyroid from working properly. Cooking these foods destroys the goitrogens making them a perfectly acceptable food.
- Supplement with zinc, selenium, tyrosine and vitamins A, E and C, all of which are needed to boost thyroid function.
- Add the yellow spice turmeric to your food, as studies have shown that this spice can help speed up thyroid activity.
- Talk to your GP, if you have severe hypothyroidism you may need to take thyroxin medication.

Action plan

- Talk to your GP or find a Nutritional Therapist in your area, and consider a Female Hormone Panel to get your hormone levels assessed.

- Make sure your bowels are regular by eating plenty of fibre and taking probiotics.

- Cut back on xenoestrogens by avoiding food in plastic containers, drinking filtered water rather than water in plastic bottles and reducing red meat and dairy products.

- Increase phytoestrogens by including soya foods and flaxseeds in your daily diet.

- Clean up your diet and lifestyle to help lighten your toxic load and improve your liver function.

- Calculate your BMI and follow a healthy eating and exercise routine to help get back into shape if you discover that you fall into the overweight or obese category.

'The type of foods you eat massively influences your state of health. If you eat foods that are fresh, natural and full of nutritional value then your body has a very good chance of being strong and healthy.'

Summing Up

▪ Hormone imbalance, low levels of transport proteins, neurotransmitter imbalance, BMI and body fat, poor liver function, constipation and having an underactive thyroid can all contribute to PMS. It may be as little as one of these factors or as many as all of these factors that are linked into your PMS.

▪ By changing your diet and lifestyle you can help correct each factor, easing your PMS.

Chapter Six

Diet and Lifestyle Factors

There are a number of diet and lifestyle factors that can influence PMS. Different systems in your body require different nutrients in order to work properly. For example, your immune system needs plenty of vitamin C, zinc and antioxidants to keep you protected from infection. Your endocrine (hormone) system also needs a handful of specific nutrients so that your hormones can be kept in balance and the glands involved can be kept nice and healthy.

A diet high in saturated fat, sugar, salt, starchy carbohydrates, processed and refined foods, and low in fruits, vegetables, oily fish, wholegrains and fibre is unlikely to give you an adequate supply of the nutrients your endocrine system needs. This is why your hormones can end up out of balance.

It's not just diet that's important, your level of fitness and level of toxicity also need to be considered. Too little exercise, and your body will be sluggish and stagnant and this will be reflected in your hormonal pattern. Too much body toxicity from caffeine, alcohol, nicotine and other social drugs, and your liver function and hormone balance will be affected. Time to shape up and clean up!

Poor diet

The type of foods you eat massively influences your state of health. If you eat foods that are fresh, natural and full of nutritional value, then your body has a very good chance of being strong and healthy. But if your diet is nutritionally imbalanced, then your body will start to show signs of weakness.

Eat lots of the right foods and you'll find that your PMS is much more bearable. Eat too many of the wrong foods and you'll find your PMS is notched up a few levels. The right foods are the ones that contain the right kinds of vitamins, minerals, fibre and good fats needed to keep your hormones in balance. The wrong foods contain a bunch of nutrients that make it very hard for hormone balance to be kept on an even keel – sugar, salt and saturated fat. You need to bear in mind that when it comes to PMS and food and nutrition, the phrase 'everything in moderation' couldn't be more applicable.

Too much sugar and refined food

Dr Abraham made the link between sugar and PMS when he discovered that women with PMS consume 275% more refined sugar than women without PMS. It's now generally accepted that PMS is far more common for women who eat a high sugar diet.

The reasons why women with PMS have such a strong relationship with sugar is still not fully understood. It seems that many of the symptoms of PMS, such as irritability, mood swings, fatigue, headaches, palpitations, sugar cravings and anxiety, are also the symptoms of hypoglycaemia, commonly known as 'low blood sugar'.

Our ancestors

Sugar (glucose) is what your body uses for fuel, providing every cell in your body with energy. Our ancestors consumed very little sugar in their diet. The main sweet foods available to them would have been seasonal fruits and honey. So where did they get their energy from? Well sugar is also part of the compound 'starch' found in many carbohydrate foods like grains, vegetables and pulses. These foods, in their natural state, also contain lots of fibre. It's this fibre that slows down the release of sugar from these foods during digestion, giving a 'sustained' release of energy that kept our ancestors energised across the day.

Sweet tooth

Our modern diet is now very different and we have developed a tendency to indulge our sweet tooth. We've managed to extract sugar from naturally sweet foods so that we can add sugar to many of the foods we eat. And with this sugar we've invented soft drinks, chocolate, sweets and puddings, all of which contain levels of sugar that far exceed what our ancestors would have consumed.

We've also learnt how to 'refine' our carbohydrate foods which means that we've taken out the fibre factor, leaving all the starch and sugar behind. This refining process has given us white pasta, white rice, white noodles, white flour, white bread and all the things that you can make from these ingredients – cakes, biscuits, pastries, croissants etc.

Sugar roller coaster

Compared to our ancestors we eat a phenomenal amount of sugar and starch and much less fibre. Our diets might have radically changed but our bodies haven't. The truth is that our body still prefers, functions better and is much more suited to the diet of our ancestors. Our high refined carbohydrate and high sugar intake hasn't done us any favours. This increase in sugar and starch can quite literally leave you on an energy and mood roller coaster.

When you eat sweet or starchy foods that don't contain lots of fibre, the sugar from these foods is released very quickly into your bloodstream giving you an initial energy and mood 'high'. Your body produces the hormone insulin which takes all this extra sugar out of the blood, tucking it safely away into body cells where it can be instantly burned for energy or saved for later use, by converting into fat.

However, if you eat too much sugar in one go, then you produce too much insulin and this triggers a blood sugar low which sends your mood and energy buzz crashing. Irritability, fatigue, headache, cravings and low mood are all signs that you have hit a sugar low. You reach for a sugar fix and up you go on that roller coaster ride again.

'When you eat sweet or starchy foods that don't contain lots of fibre, the sugar from these foods is released very quickly into your bloodstream giving you an initial energy and mood "high".'

Sugar and PMS

This massive increase in dietary sugar and starch can play havoc with your hormone levels. Studies have shown that during the luteal (premenstrual) phase of their cycle, women with PMS-C have a tendency to produce far too much insulin when they eat sweet or starchy foods, which causes their blood sugar levels to fall far too low after they have eaten. This is why these women experience the symptoms of hypoglycaemia – sugar cravings, mood swings, tearfulness, anxiety, palpitations, shakes, edginess, irritability and headaches.

Sugar Tracker Chart

For one month record how many times each day you eat foods that contain sugar. You could be in for a surprise! For example if on day three you drank four cups of tea containing added sugar then score 4 in this box. On day six if you ate two chocolate bars then score 2 in this box.

Day	Added sugar to cereal or hot drinks	Honey or syrup	Jam or marmalade	Fruit juice	Soft drinks	Cakes	Biscuits	Chocolate	Sweets	Puddings	Pastries
1											
2											
3											
4											
5											
6											
7											
8											
9											
10											
11											
12											
13											
14											
15											
16											
17											
18											
19											
20											
21											
22											
23											
24											
25											
26											
27											
28											
Total											

Need2Know

The more sugar and refined carbohydrate foods that you eat, the more this insulin high followed by a sugar low is likely to happen, so cutting back on sugar and starchy foods is essential if you want to step off the monthly sugar and mood roller coaster.

Sugar watch

Scientists have also discovered that low levels of serotonin, linked with women with PMS-D, trigger sugar cravings. Women tend to have an emotional link with sugary foods and the lower your serotonin levels the stronger your emotional link will be. If you want to cut back on sugar then start taking note of how you feel when you reach for your sugar fix. Once you know your emotional triggers then you can take steps to make different choices.

Emotional reasons to reach for sugar foods:

- Happy.
- Angry.
- Bored.
- Lonely.
- Tired.
- Disappointed.
- Self-hatred.
- Rejected.
- Need a reward.

Making changes

- You only need 90g of sugar a day, so start looking at labels for all your foods, drinks and sweet treats. You'll soon find out how quickly you reach your 90g limit.

- Think you don't eat much sugar? Double check this theory. For one month record how many sweet foods and drinks you consume by recording your daily intake of fruit juice, soft drinks, added sugar to hot drinks, sweets, chocolate, cakes, biscuits, pastries etc. Use the Sugar Tracker Chart to help you.

- Check out what your refined carbohydrate status is. Take note of whether you buy white bread, white rice, white pasta, white noodles, white flour, croissants and pastry, and start to swap to the wholegrain alternatives as these contain the fibre factor that will get you off that sugar roller coaster. Use the Carbohydrate Checklist to help you.

- Get on top of your emotions – think about how you feel when you reach for a sugar fix.

Carbohydrate Checklist

To find out whether you are eating too many foods that are rich in sugar and starch and not enough of the healthy low sugar, high fibre carbohydrates then simply complete this carbohydrate checklist. All you have to do is put a tick by the foods that you buy regularly. Add up the ticks in each column to reveal if you eat more unhealthy refined carbohydrates that healthy unrefined carbohydrates!

Unhealthy Carbohydrate Foods:

☐ Breakfast cereals.

☐ Sugar coated breakfast cereals.

☐ Croissants.

☐ White bread.

☐ White bagels.

☐ White pitta.

☐ White rice.

☐ White pasta

☐ White noodles.

☐ White flour.

☐ White English muffins.

☐ Crumpets.

☐ Pancakes.

☐ Pastries.

☐ Biscuits.

☐ Cakes.

☐ Chocolate.

☐ Sweets.

Total

Healthy Unrefined Carbohydrates:

☐ Unsweetened Swiss style muesli.

☐ Porridge oats.

☐ Wholegrain bread.

☐ Wholegrain bagels.

☐ Wholegrain pitta.

☐ Wholegrain rice.

☐ Wholegrain pasta.

☐ Brown rice noodles.

☐ Wild rice.

☐ Buckwheat noodles.

☐ Wholegrain flour.

☐ Wholegrain English muffins.

☐ Wholegrain cereal bars.

☐ Healthy Low GI oat bars

☐ Quinoa.

☐ Millet.

☐ Buckwheat flour.

☐ Pulses.

☐ Lentils.

Total

Too much salt

The problem with salt is that it makes food taste delicious! But the more you add, the more you get accustomed too, so it's very easy to end up eating more salt than you need. If you cut back on salt then at first your food can taste very bland, but after just a couple of weeks your taste buds adapt and it's not long before you can taste the natural flavour of your food again.

If you suffer from water retention during the premenstrual phase of your cycle, then sprinkling salt all over your food is only going to exacerbate these symptoms. The more salt you add the more sodium your body will retain and the puffier your hands, face, feet and ankles will become. Your breasts will be more swollen and tender too.

'If you suffer from water retention during the premenstrual phase of your cycle, then sprinkling salt all over your food is only going to exacerbate these symptoms.'

You might be reading this thinking 'well I get these symptoms but I don't add any salt to my plate'. If this is the case then you need to look at how much salt you add to your food during cooking or you need to look for 'hidden' salt in the foods that you buy. Processed foods like ready meals, prepared sandwiches, cook-in sauces and even bread, pickles, olives, ham, cured meats and bacon contain heaps of salt. Chips, crisps, cheese biscuits, salted nuts and other salty snacks are also packed with salt.

Making changes

- You only need 6g of salt a day, so start to look at labels and see how much extra salt you are getting from processed foods.

- Take the salt shaker off the table.

- Swap your sea salt for a 'low-sodium' salt, as this means you can still season your food without your sodium levels getting too high.

- Swap salty snacks for alternatives such as vegetable crudities and hummus or simply fresh fruit.

Too much saturated fat

Saturated fats are naturally occurring fats found in red meat, butter, milk, cheese, lard, cream, yoghurt and ice cream. This also means that foods made from these ingredients are also high in saturated fat – cakes, biscuits, puddings, pastry, milk chocolate, sausages, hams and preserved meats.

Prostaglandin link

If you make a big effort to cut back on these foods or even cut them out of your diet completely for a few months, then you'll be amazed at how many of your 'painful' symptoms will start to just disappear. The reason for this is that saturated fats get converted by your body into 'pro-inflammatory' prostaglandins, which your body uses to increase pain and inflammation. Having too many of these pro-inflammatory prostaglandins has been found to make breast tissue more sensitive and reduce levels of serotonin, your 'happy' brain chemical.

Studies show that reducing saturated fat helps to reduce the amount of oestrogen circulating around your body by as much as 36%. A good tip if you suffer from PMS-A and PMS-H.

Foods that are naturally high in saturated fat also tend to be high in xenoestrogens. So cutting back on saturated fat also helps reduce your exposure to these potent and harmful synthetic hormones.

'Saturated fats get converted by your body into 'pro-inflammatory' prostaglandins, which your body uses to increase pain and inflammation.'

Making changes

▨ You shouldn't be eating more that 20g of saturated fat a day and less is best.

▨ The easiest way to reduce saturated fat in your diet is to swap animal and dairy foods for healthier options. Swap red meat to white meat or to fish. Use skimmed or semi-skimmed milk or switch to soya milk. Take a break from cheese, healthier sandwich options include hummus, tuna, salmon, turkey or chicken. Swap butter for an olive oil, soya or vegetable oil spread. Choose spreads that are free from harmful trans fats and hydrogenated fats.

▨ Choose a natural 'probiotic' or 'live' low fat or no fat yoghurt or soya yoghurt.

▨ When buying ready meals always check the label for the saturated fat content.

Too much caffeine

Drinking too much tea, coffee and energy drinks can heighten your symptoms of PMS, particularly anxiety, irritability, agitation, breast tenderness, depression, poor sleep and palpitations. These drinks contain caffeine and other 'methylxanthines' which activate stress hormones and encourage fluid retention and worsen breast lumps. Cutting back on caffeine can greatly help to reduce the severity of your symptoms.

Making changes

- Limit tea and coffee to just one cup a day.

- There are also lots of caffeine-free alternatives to coffee including Barley cup, Yannoh and Dandelion coffee.

- Ditch energy drinks for mineral water with a splash of fruit juice.

- Try different herbal teas to see which ones you like. Dr Stuart's, Pukka, Heath and Heather, Higher Living and Yogi teas are all good brands with lots of different flavour combinations to choose from. Good herbal tea options for PMS include:

    - Fennel – helps with water retention.

    - Cinnamon – helps with sugar cravings.

    - Nettle – helps with detox.

    - Chamomile – helps calm anxiety.

    - Peppermint – helps with period pain.

    - Liquorice – helps with water retention.

Not enough fibre

According to the World Health Organisation (WHO), we should be eating five pieces (over 400g) of fruit and vegetables a day in order to stay healthy. However, it's been estimated that as few as 12% of the UK population manage to hit the 5-a-day target, which means that many of us just aren't getting enough fibre. There are two main reasons why fibre is important in the prevention of PMS.

- Eating foods high in fibre improves blood sugar balance. Wholegrains, lentils, pulses, vegetables and some fruits tend to have a low GI (glycaemic index – which you'll learn more about later) and it's these foods that help to normalise insulin levels, good news for hormone balance. So eating foods high in fibre helps to smooth over those sugar and mood highs and lows.

- Fibre helps to remove waste hormones from your body. Your liver is in charge of packing up hormones ready for excretion. Once packaged these bundles of waste hormones bind with fibre in your intestine and hitch a ride out of the body. If you don't have enough fibre in your diet then your discarded hormones get reabsorbed back into your body, sending your hormone levels sky high.

Too much alcohol

Studies have shown that women with PMS drink more alcohol before their period than women without PMS. Some experts believe that women with PMS drink to help them cope with their symptoms, but there are other possible reasons. Progesterone levels naturally drop during your premenstrual phase (7-10 days before your period) and these low levels of progesterone are thought to enhance cravings for alcohol and decrease alcohol tolerance.

One thing's for sure, alcohol and PMS don't mix. You might think that a few drinks will help take the edge off your symptoms, but the reality is that alcohol is a mood depressant and drinking during the luteal phase of your cycle can cause your mood and energy to plummet.

'It's been estimated that as few as 12% of the UK population manage to hit the 5-a-day target, which means that many of us just aren't getting enough fibre.'

Alcohol also causes blood sugar levels to drop, which can be unfavourable for women with PMS-C whose blood sugar levels are already challenged. This is why drinking alcohol encourages PMS symptoms of mood swings, irritability, cravings and headaches. Drinking too much alcohol has also been linked to premenstrual breast tenderness.

If you are a heavy drinker then this will interfere with your liver function, affecting your ability to clear excessive hormones from your body, potentially leaving you with hormone imbalance.

Making changes

- The guidelines for alcohol for women in the UK is 14 units a week. The advice that I give to my clients with PMS is to cut back to three glasses of wine a week – that's one glass of wine a day, on three different days of the week. Not three glasses of wine on one day of the week.

- Binge drinking has a far greater impact on hormone imbalance than drinking a little, often. So don't save your units up for the weekend, especially if the weekend falls 7-10 days before your period.

- If you are a heavy drinker then get help and support so that you can get your alcohol consumption in check.

Lack of exercise

Research shows that women who exercise regularly have PMS less frequently than women who lead sedentary lifestyles. Studies have also shown that women who partake in regular or a high level of exercise report fewer PMS symptoms and suffer less from low mood, poor concentration, mood swings, anxiety and pain.

We've all got the message that exercise is good for us, but many of us still use common excuses that stop us committing to a regular exercise routine. I frequently hear many of my clients say that they're 'too tired, that joining a gym or a class costs too much, that they are too self-conscious about their

'Research shows that women who exercise regularly have PMS less frequently than women who lead sedentary lifestyles.'

body shape, that exercising is too painful or that they are too embarrassed about their level of fitness'. Well ladies, the bad news is that unless you start exercising, your PMS will continue or get worse!

Exercise is important not just for PMS but also for your cardiovascular fitness, vitally and longevity. It really is time to get over your insecurities and ditch your excuses. Find something that you enjoy and build this into your daily or weekly routine, whichever works best for you. Keep it simple so it doesn't become stressful.

Exercise helps prevent PMS

▨ Exercise stimulates your liver to produce transport proteins such as SHBG, which helps maintain hormone balance.

▨ Exercise raises endorphins and serotonin, boosting your mood and reducing pain and inflammation.

▨ Exercise helps burn fat and helps you achieve and maintain a healthy BMI, lowering your oestrogenic load.

▨ Exercise helps you feel positive about your body image.

Making changes

▨ If you like exercising on your own then you might find that the gym, spin classes, or jogging work well for you.

▨ If you want exercise to be free then start walking daily and as your fitness improves step up the pace until you reach a comfortable jog.

▨ If you need a little support to get started then partner up with a fitness buddy for tennis, badminton, hockey, netball, basketball or even football. Do an online search for clubs in your area.

▨ If you love music and dancing then sign up to a dance class, zumba or a fitness class.

- If you have joint aches and pains that prevent you from exercise then try swimming, as the water helps to take the weight of your body, aqua-aerobics or even chair yoga.
- Take the advice of a Personal Trainer who can assess your level of fitness and put together a plan that is realistic and achievable.

Action plan

- Cut back on foods containing sugar and refined carbohydrates. Start including more fibre in your diet by achieving your 5-a-day, every day.
- Cut back on saturated fat by swapping red meat for chicken, turkey or fish and reducing cheese and other dairy products.
- Cut back on salt by avoiding adding salt to your food and cutting back on salty snacks.
- Limit drinks containing caffeine to one per day and avoid energy drinks.
- Cut back on alcohol to three glasses of wine a week (one glass, three days out of the week) or at least get back to 14 units a week.
- Commit to three 30-60 minute exercise sessions a week. It's important that you find something that you enjoy and that feels right for you.

Summing Up

▨ It's true that many of your symptoms exist as a result of hormone imbalance but it's important to realise that your hormone imbalance is merely a reflection of poor diet and a toxic or stagnant lifestyle.

▨ By taking steps to reduce sugar, saturated fat, caffeine, salt and alcohol and replacing these with fresh, nutritionally balanced foods, your hormones will start to come back into balance.

▨ The changes you make now will help protect you from symptoms in your next cycle and beyond.

Chapter Seven

Good Nutrition

If I've learnt anything during my years of clinical practice, it's the observation that given the right foods in the right proportions the human body has an incredible capacity to be able to recover from illness. PMS is a condition that reflects a diet and lifestyle that's gone wayward. Like other hormonal conditions, PMS responds very well to nutritional intervention. By tweaking your nutrient intake, balancing your fats and by including a few special phytonutrients, you'll be able to get your hormones back in balance and your symptoms of PMS under control.

GI diet

Since dietary sugars, refined carbohydrates and low blood sugar all have a part to play in PMS, particularly for women with PMS-C, then following a style of eating that focuses on balancing blood sugar makes complete sense for PMS. This is why the GI diet has fast become the diet of choice for women wanting to address their PMS. So what does GI mean?

GI stands for gylcaemic index, and this is a number that expresses how fast and how much your blood sugar levels are expected to rise after eating foods containing carbohydrates (sugar and starch). The glycaemic index was formulated by nutritionist Dr David Jenkins in 1981, and it runs from a scale of 0 to 100. To make it easy, the GI diet splits carbohydrate foods into three categories, each with a set range of GI scores:

- High GI – foods that have a GI value above 70.

- Moderate GI – foods that have a GI value between 55-69.

- Low GI – foods that have a GI value of less than 55.

'The GI diet has fast become the diet of choice for women wanting to address their PMS.'

High GI foods

We now know that foods containing lots of sugar or starch and very little fibre release sugar very quickly into the bloodstream. This sharp rise in sugar is very stressful for the body and the quick high is shortly followed by an uncomfortable blood sugar low which triggers symptoms of anxiety, cravings, palpitations, irritability, headaches and mood swings. Foods that have a high GI value are the ones that need to be avoided, as these foods trigger blood sugar highs and lows and are likely to keep you on that sugar roller coaster.

High GI foods include:

- Pulses – broad beans.
- Grains – breakfast cereals (cornflakes, sultana bran, branflakes, Coco Pops, puffed rice, puffed wheat, Cheerios, Weetabix), white bread, baguettes, corn chips, pretzels, white rice, water crackers, Ryvita, rice cakes, puffed crisp breads.
- Fruits – grapes, melons, dates, raisins.
- Vegetables – carrots, parsnips, pumpkins, baked potato, mashed potatoes, chips, cooked beetroot
- Other – alcohol, sugar, fizzy soft drinks, biscuits, donuts, scones.

Moderate GI Foods

Foods with a moderate GI value still activate the sugar roller coaster but the highs and lows are less pronounced. These foods have a much gentler impact on blood sugar levels when compared to the high GI foods. If the carbohydrate portion of your diet is made up just from moderate GI foods then you are still likely to experience blood sugar highs and lows and PMS. It's highly recommended that the majority of your carbohydrates come from low GI foods with an allowance for a few moderated GI foods every now and again.

Moderate GI foods include:

- Pulses – split peas, kidney beans, baked beans.

- Grains – buckwheat, wholemeal bread, rye crackers, popcorn, white pasta, no added sugar muesli, pastry, white basmati rice.
- Fruits – kiwi, mango, peaches, pineapple.
- Vegetables – boiled potatoes, peas, carrots, sweetcorn.
- Dairy – Ice cream.
- Other – honey, less than 70% chocolate, crisps.

Low GI foods

Low GI foods contain plenty of fibre and are low in sugar and starch. Low GI foods release sugar into the bloodstream very slowly and because of this are considered to have a 'sustained' effect on mood and energy, a big plus for PMS sufferers. By swapping high GI foods for more low GI foods you enable your body to maintain healthy blood sugar levels across the day. This is a great way to overcome sugar cravings, binge eating and sugar addiction as you quite literally put the brakes on your sugar roller coaster. By smoothing over the highs and lows your hormones settle back into balance and your sugar-related PMS symptoms should start to clear.

Low GI foods include:

- Pulses – lentils, butter beans, chick peas, audiki beans, cannellini beans, black eye beans, split peas.
- Nuts – hazelnuts, almonds, pecans, walnuts, pistachio, macadamia, pine nuts.
- Seeds – pumpkin, sesame, flax, sunflower.
- Grains – amaranth, brown rice, barley, millet, oats, oatcakes, quinoa, rye bread, wholewheat pasta.
- Fruits – apple juice, apples, apricots, dried apricots, berries, cherries, grapefruit, oranges, pears, plums.
- Vegetables – sweet potato, broccoli, cabbage, onions, spinach and other green vegetables, lettuce and other salad greens, green beans, mushrooms and peppers

- Dairy – milk, natural yoghurt.
- Other – 70% cocoa chocolate.

Three GI rules

The basic rule of thumb for the GI diet to be successful is to follow these guidelines:

- Avoid or limit your consumption of high GI foods (value higher than 70).
- Eat a moderate amount of moderate GI foods (value of 55-69).
- Consume an abundance of low GI foods (value less than 55).

Susie says:

'When I first started working as a Nutritional Therapist I was surprised at how quickly women responded to a GI diet. It soon became apparent that by focusing on a GI diet alone, clients would experience a radical and positive change in their PMS within just 1-2 cycles. It became quite typical for me to hear clients say on return visits, "It's amazing I didn't even know my period was due this month as I didn't get my normal moody warning signs". I'm now a firm believer that following a GI diet is a good place to start if you want to address your PMS. Once this diet is in place, you might have just a few core symptoms left to work with.'

Benefits of the GI diet:

- Helps reduce PMS, especially symptoms belonging to the PMS-C profile.
- Easy way to achieve your 5-a-day.
- Promotes bowel function and healthy digestion.
- Reduces sugar and starchy food cravings.
- Helps to crack a sugar addiction.

From GI to GL

It's been a few years since Dr Jenkins introduced the GI concept. Although this is a highly successful diet, scientists and nutritionists have recently brought attention to a GI flaw. You might have noticed that some unhealthy foods appear in the moderate or low GI categories. For example, we all know that (as much as we love it) ice cream is a very unhealthy food, high in saturated fat and sugar, yet it appears in the moderate GI list.

Research has shown that like fibre, fat also slows down the release of sugar into the bloodstream. This is why foods high in sugar and fat don't tend to appear in the high GI category even though they contain heaps of sugar and are considered to be unhealthy foods.

You might also have noticed that some very healthy foods, mainly some fruits and vegetables (carrots, parsnips, cooked beetroot, baked potato, grapes, melon, broad beans) appear in the high GI list. There is no reason to limit these foods, especially if you want to achieve your 5-a-day.

So the GL (glycaemic load) diet was invented to fix these flaws. The GL diet takes the GI value and relates it to the portion size of a food. For example, 100g of ice cream is far more detrimental to your blood sugar levels and your health than 100g of parsnips! The GL system has allowed the GI diet to evolve to exclude unhealthy foods and include healthy foods.

Making changes

▨ Start to be aware of the types of GI foods you buy when you go shopping.

▨ Start to make easy swaps from high GI foods to low GI foods.

▨ If you are eating out or buying snacks then get into the habit of thinking about the GI concept. It won't take long for you to remember which foods have a healthy low GI.

▨ Always choose a wholegrain (brown) option over a refined (white) option.

▨ Swapping white bread, pasta and rice for wholegrain alternatives has a very positive impact on blood sugar balance and PMS.

Vegetarian diet

There's a lot of scientific evidence to suggest that a vegetarian diet helps to address PMS. This is no great surprise if you think of the foods that you are likely to cut out of your diet when you become vegetarian. Meat contains saturated fat and hormone residues which can tip your natural hormone balance out of kilter. Going vegetarian might sound like a temping solution for your PMS but it depends on your interpretation of 'vegetarian'.

If you're the type of vegetarian that lives off cheese on toast and pizza, doesn't like fresh vegetables or pulses and likes to snack on crisps, chips and chocolate, then becoming vegetarian isn't going to shift your PMS, in fact it might even make it worse!

'Meat contains saturated fat and hormone residues which can tip your natural hormone balance out of kilter.'

However, if you are prepared to embrace a nutritionally balanced vegetarian diet which incorporates plenty of wholegrains, pulses, nuts, seeds, soya products (milk, yoghurt, tofu, miso), seaweeds, sprouts, superfoods, vegetables and fruits, then you'll reap the rewards of your culinary efforts. The key to successful reduction in PMS through a balanced vegetarian diet is to remember that dairy products, in particular cheese, need to be kept to a minimum.

If giving up fleshy foods is just one step too far for you then there is a great deal of symptom relief to be achieved from a wholesome vegetarian diet with the addition of fish either daily or 3-4 times a week.

Making changes

- Start to swap your red and white meat for fish.
- Consider having more vegetarian meals.
- Buy a vegetarian cook book for culinary inspiration.
- Include more superfoods, sprouts and pulses in your diet.

Phytoestrogens

Nature tends to graciously provide us with everything we need to achieve good health, and when it comes to hormone balance we need to look at a group of natural substances called phytoestrogens found in many foods. Phytoestrogens are very clever because they help to 'normalise' the amount of oestrogen activity in your body. If your natural levels of oestrogen are too low then these phytoestrogens will help to boost oestrogen activity. If your oestrogen levels have climbed too high, as seen with PMS-H and PMS-A, then these clever phytoestrogens help to dampen down oestrogen activity.

Including phytoestrogens in your diet can help to improve oestrogen balance and soften some of your oestrogen-related symptoms. Soya foods are known to contain the highest levels of phytoestrogens, and when soya foods are fermented these phytoestrogens become even more powerful and helpful for hormone balance.

Asian diets contain high levels of soya foods and scientists think this is why countries like China and Japan have very low incidences of oestrogen-related conditions such as PMS, menopausal symptoms, breast cancer and osteoporosis.

'Phytoestrogens are very clever because they help to "normalise" the amount of oestrogen activity in your body.'

Foods that contain phytoestrogens

- Soya foods – soya milk, tofu, edamame beans and fermented soya foods – miso, tempeh, soya yogurt, soy sauce.

- Nuts and seeds – flaxseeds, sesame seeds, sunflower seeds, almonds, chestnuts, peanuts.

- Pulses and wholegrains – mung beans, alfalfa sprouts, chickpeas (hummus), lentils, oats, rice.

- Fruits – dried dates, dried apricots, apples, blueberries.

- Vegetables – fennel, cucumber, green beans, garlic, onion, yam.

Making changes

- Swap cows' milk to soya milk and also make the change to soya yoghurt.

- Add a teaspoon of miso to soups, stews or stir-fries.

- Drizzle soya sauce over rice or use with 'five spice', olive oil and rice wine vinegar to make an Asian style dressing for salads.

- Snack on edamame beans and phytoestrogen-rich seeds and nuts.

Vitamins and minerals

Ask any nutritionist which nutrients are important for hormone balance and the answer you'll get is – vitamins B6 and E, zinc and magnesium. These nutrients are used by the ovaries to make oestrogen and progesterone and they are also needed to maintain the health of the glands that keep your hormone cycle in sync. Another nutrient that is much less talked about, but that's equally important for PMS, is chromium.

Women with PMS tend to have low levels of vitamin B6 and magnesium, and studies have found these nutrients positively affect many symptoms of PMS, particularly the mood-related symptoms. Supplementing with vitamin B6 has been found to help correct oestrogen and progesterone imbalance. However, it's thought that some women are unable to convert vitamin B6 into its active form, so supplementing with the active form called pyridoxal-5-phospate or P-5-P is of great importance.

Helpful nutrients for PMS:

- Vitamin E – helps with breast tenderness, anxiety, fatigue, depression, insomnia.

- Vitamin B6 – hormone balance and many mood-related symptoms, premenstrual acne, good for all PMS profiles.

- Magnesium – stress, anxiety, water retention, fatigue, aches and pains, breast tenderness, weight gain, hormone balance, particularly good for PMS-H and PMS-D.

- Zinc – helps to reduce prolactin, particularly helpful for PMS-A.

- Chromium – helps with blood sugar balance, sugar cravings, mood swings, irritability, headaches, palpitations and is particularly useful for PMS-C.

Food sources of helpful PMS nutrients

Vitamin B6	Vitamin E	Zinc	Magnesium	Chromium
milk	sunflower seeds	oysters	figs	oysters
lean meats	almonds and hazelnuts	lean meat	buckwheat	fish
banana	avocados	fish	green vegetables	lean meat
pulses	wheat and oat germ	pumpkin seeds	almonds	wholegrains and bran
brown rice	fish	peanuts	cashews	liver
prunes	green vegetables	split peas	pulses	nuts

'Women with PMS tend to have low levels of vitamin B6 and magnesium, and studies have found these nutrients to positively affect many symptoms of PMS, particularly the mood-related symptoms.'

Making changes

▨ By including more of the foods that are rich in these helpful nutrients, you'll start to provide your body with the ingredients needed to maintain hormone balance.

▨ It's important to get the correct advice about nutritional supplements, don't just self-prescribe. Visit the www.bant.org.uk website to find a Nutritional Therapist in your area.

▨ Most of the supplement companies have a 'nutrition' or 'technical' department that you can telephone and talk with an expert for advice on which nutrients to supplement and at what dosage, this service is normally free.

Good fats

One of the main dietary imbalances associated with PMS is too much saturated fat and not enough of the good 'omega' fats. As explained in chapter 6, too much saturated fat is bad for PMS, as it leads to increased oestrogen levels and increased pain and inflammation. Cutting back on foods high in saturated fat is a good start, but what really makes the difference to symptoms is to also increase your intake of omega-3 fats.

These 'good' fats are found in oily fish, some nuts and seeds, and can help to calm down 'painful' symptoms. They can also help increase concentration and memory and improve brain function and mood.

Foods rich in omega-3

▨ Oily fish – salmon, mackerel, fresh tuna, trout, herrings, pilchards and sardines.

▨ Nuts – walnuts.

▨ Seeds – hemp, chia, flax.

Top-up on GLA

Omega-6 fats are also 'good' fats found in many nuts, seeds and vegetables. Your body uses enzymes, which rely on vitamin B6, zinc and magnesium to work properly, to convert these omega-6 fats into GLA (gamma linolenic acid). Women with PMS have been found to have low levels of GLA and this is thought to trigger symptoms of breast tenderness and water retention.

Numerous studies highlight the fact that women with PMS tend to have low levels of vitamin B6, zinc and magnesium and experts believe that these nutrient deficiencies cause the GLA deficiency. Eating foods rich in vitamin B6, zinc and magnesium can help, as can taking a supplement of these three nutrients. There are a good number of studies that show that supplementing with GLA can help to improve PMS and alleviate breast tenderness.

Supplements containing GLA:

- Evening primrose oil.
- Blackcurrant seed oil.
- Borage oil, also known as starflower oil.

Making changes

- Cut back on red meat, fried foods, cheese, butter, cream, ice cream, preserved meats and other foods high in saturated fat.
- Increase oily fish to 3-4 times a week, which helps improve your levels of omega-3 fats needed for good skin, hormone balance and mood.
- Snack on nuts and seeds to help improve your intake of the 'good' omega fats.
- Consider supplementing with GLA for 1-3 months.

Mood-boosting tryptophan

Low levels of serotonin, the brain chemical responsible for 'happy' feelings is at the route of many of the mood-related symptoms of PMS, and this is particularly true for PMS-D and PDD. Serotonin is made from a type of protein called tryptophan found in certain foods. By increasing these foods in your diet you can help provide your body with the raw ingredients needed to boost serotonin levels.

Foods rich in tryptophan:

- Egg white.
- Turkey.
- Chicken.
- Fish.
- Cottage cheese.
- Yoghurt.
- Peanuts.
- Oats.
- Pumpkin seeds.

Making changes

- Start to include more tryptophan foods in your diet.
- Make sure you get some 'outdoor' time every day, as this also encourages your body to make serotonin.
- Sleep pattern is important too. The more you stick to a healthy sleep routine of 'early to bed and early to rise' the easier it is for your body to top-up on serotonin.
- Exercise helps to boost serotonin so make sure you commit to 2-3 cardiovascular exercise sessions a week.

Need2Know

Cruciferous vegetables

In recent years cruciferous vegetables have been highlighted as being important for hormone balance. According to researchers this family of vegetables contains a natural substance called 'indoles' which help the liver process and clear out oestrogen. This is why women with PMS and other hormone-related conditions are being advised to increase their intake of broccoli, Brussels sprouts, cabbage, kale and cauliflower.

Making changes

- Add a portion of steamed broccoli, kale, cabbage, Brussels sprouts or cauliflower to your main meals.

- Supplement with DIM or indole-3-carbinol to help your liver clear out excess oestrogen level.

Action plan

- Take some time to look into the GI and GL diet and find ways to accommodate this style of eating into your meal planning and shopping.

- Consider following a diet that includes more healthy vegetarian meals to help increase fibre and reduce saturated fat.

- Cut back on saturated fat and increase oily fish and nuts and seeds to help get your fat balance favourable for clearing PMS.

- Look at the list of foods rich in helpful nutrients of PMS. Pick out the ones that you know you like and start to include these in your diet.

- To help hormone balance include foods rich in phytoestrogens and cruciferous vegetables.

- If you are feeling low or suffer from premenstrual depression then increase tryptophan-rich foods.

- Talk to a Nutritional Therapist about which supplements you should take, this is a great way to get a personalised supplement programme, one that's designed to clear your specific symptoms of PMS.

Summing Up

- Changing your diet and getting used to shopping for new foods, cooking with different ingredients and adjusting to new tastes and flavours can seem overwhelming at first.

- It's important to make changes at a pace that suits you so you don't feel stressed by all the new aspects of your diet. Just look at the list of action points and change the ones that feel easy first. When you have acclimatised to this then re-look at the list and see which ones you can change next.

- Once you have made all the changes then you can relax and stick to the 80:20 rule and this way you'll be making plenty of progress. Don't beat yourself up if you have a couple of indulgent days, this is perfectly normal. By following the 80:20 rule you can be good 80% of the time and you can 'relax the rules' 20% of the time. This is helpful if you have celebrations or social events booked in the diary.

Chapter Eight

Natural Therapies and Remedies

In previous chapters you've read all about the types of diet and lifestyle changes you should make to free yourself from PMS. However, some women find it hard to make changes on their own. Having a course of treatments can provide you with a great deal of support. Natural therapies are of great benefit and can help to restore hormone balance and correct PMS.

Nutritional therapy

Nutritional therapy can help with an almost endless list of health conditions and symptoms. Your family may have a predisposed risk factor for hormone-related conditions like PMS, but by changing your diet and taking certain supplements you can start to reduce your risk of developing PMS.

The main focus of nutritional therapy is to get your overall balance of dietary fats, proteins, carbohydrates, fibre and water in the right proportions for you as an individual. It's so easy to stick to the same types of foods all through your life. But small dietary imbalances in the short term can lead to larger deficiencies or excesses in the long term. This can eventually get expressed as symptoms, conditions or even actual diagnosed diseases.

Supportive supplements and PMS

There are a number of good quality nutritional supplements that contain herbs, vitamins, minerals and phytonutrients which can be used to help with hormone balance and PMS:

'The main focus of nutritional therapy is to get your overall balance of dietary fats, proteins, carbohydrates, fibre and water in the right proportions for you as an individual.'

- General PMS support – vitamins B6 and E, zinc and magnesium.
- Sugar cravings – chromium, cinnamon.
- Breast tenderness – GLA, liquorice.
- Low progesterone – Agnus castus.
- Oestrogen imbalance – soy-isoflavones.
- High oestrogen – DIM, indole-3-carbinol, calcium D-glucarate.
- High testosterone – saw palmetto.
- Stress – magnesium, rhodiola, gingseng.
- Depression – 5-HTP, St John's wort.
- Anxiety – L-theanine, calcium, magnesium.
- Liver support – milk thistle, artichoke, dandelion, inositol, choline, methionine, MSM, glutathione.
- Thyroid support – kelp, guggul gum, selenium.

Trusted brands

There are lots of supplement companies that sell ranges of herbs, vitamins, minerals and phytonutrients, but when it comes to supplements you tend to get what you pay for. Don't be tempted by cheap brands as these generally contain vitamins and minerals in forms that are poorly absorbed by the body and may even contain lots of fillers. There are a handful of very good brands that I recommend to my clients because they contain nutrients at good levels and in forms that the body can easily absorb. These brands include:

- BioCare – www.biocare.co.uk
- Solgar – www.solgar.co.uk
- Nutri – www.nutri-online1.co.uk
- Nutri-Link – www.nutri-linkltd.co.uk
- Higher Nature – www.highernature.co.uk

What to expect

Nutritional therapy encompasses individual prescriptions for diet and lifestyle to alleviate or prevent ailments and to promote optimal health. We are all individuals with different bodies, lifestyles and demands, which can make change easy for some and more difficult for others. A good Nutritional Therapist will take into account your needs and circumstances to formulate a simple diet and lifestyle plan with realistic goals to help you regain hormone balance.

After booking you will receive a nutrition questionnaire and food diary to complete and take with you to your initial consultation. During the appointment you'll be asked questions about your health history, diet and lifestyle. Your Nutritional Therapist will explain the factors that are contributing to your PMS and put together an action plan containing diet and lifestyle suggestions to help you overcome your symptoms. You'll also receive supplement recommendations to help with hormone balance.

A follow-up appointment, usually four weeks after your initial consultation, is used to assess your progress. Your action plan will be developed, new goals will be set and your supplements will also be reviewed.

Finding a Nutritional Therapist

The British Association for Nutritional Therapists (BANT) maintains a register of fully qualified nutritional therapists in the UK, who have the relevant professional insurance, abide by a code of ethics and keep themselves updated with CPD (continued professional development) training. Visit www.bant.org.uk and use their practitioner search facility to find a nutritional therapist in your area.

Acupuncture

Traditional acupuncture is a branch of traditional Chinese medicine – a tried and tested healthcare system that has been practised for thousands of years in China and the Far East. Acupuncture views pain and illness as a sign that the body is out of balance. What makes this system so uniquely suited to modern life is that the physical, emotional and mental sections of the body are seen as interdependent.

Energy flow

The system of acupuncture embraces the philosophy that all aspects of bodily functions are regulated by the flow of an energy-like entity called qi (pounced chee). It's acknowledged that qi flows around the body via specific energy channels called meridians which pass though different areas of the body delivering qi to specific organs and cells along the way. There are 12 main meridians – heart, spleen, kidney, liver, stomach, lung, bladder, small intestine, large intestine, gall bladder, pericardium (or heart protector) and triple heater – which an acupuncturist will assess and rebalance.

Acupuncturists believe that ill health occurs when the body's qi is unable to flow freely around the body. There can be many reasons for this – emotional and physical stress, poor nutrition, infection or injury are among the most common. These factors can cause a specific meridian to have either too much or too little qi flowing through it.

Restoring balance

The overall aim of an acupuncture treatment is to restore the body's energy equilibrium. Acupuncture aims to correct imbalances in the flow of Qi. By inserting ultra-fine sterile needles into specific acupuncture points along meridian lines that are out of balance, you reestablish the free flow of qi facilitating the body's natural healing response.

What to expect

Your acupuncturist will ask questions about your symptoms and medical history to gain a thorough understanding of your PMS, your general health and your lifestyle. Your acupuncturist will also take your pulse on both wrists and may examine your tongue to diagnose which meridians are out of balance. Your acupuncturist will then use very fine single-use pre-sterilised needles to stimulate specific acupuncture points on your body to rebalance the flow of qi.

Susie talks to acupuncturist Elaine Cook

I have found that many of my clients have benefitted from nutritional therapy in combination with acupuncture. It's a perfect marriage – nutritional therapy helps you correct your diet and lifestyle and acupuncture helps restore energy flow to the reproductive area and recharges other depleted body areas and glands.

I worked at the Dyke Road Natural Health Clinic for a number of years where I met Elaine Cook, a renowned acupuncturist with a wealth of experience, dedicated to helping women regain hormone balance. I asked Elaine to explain how acupuncture can help women with PMS and here's what she said:

'Acupuncture has been used to treat the symptoms of PMS for thousands of years and there are some common patterns seen in PMS. The liver, spleen, heart and kidney meridians and organs are most often involved in diagnosis and treatment with acupuncture for PMS.

'In Chinese medicine, the liver controls the flow of qi and blood in the body, when this is running freely the changes in hormone levels are negotiated smoothly. Emotional stress particularly affects the liver, causing the qi to stagnate, although prolonged drug use (prescription or recreational), including the oral contraceptive pill can also be a factor. Stagnation of the liver qi can cause symptoms such as headaches, anger and intense mood swings. The liver meridian travels through the reproductive organs so stagnation in the pelvis can cause abdominal pain and painful periods. Breast pain can also be due to impaired flow of liver qi.

'The spleen is responsible for the production of blood in traditional Chinese medicine, and can be vulnerable to deficiency, causing symptoms such as tiredness, dizziness, loose bowels, dry skin, insomnia, foggy headedness and poor memory. The cause of blood deficiency is often erratic eating habits. Cold or greasy foods and dairy products can damage the spleen and cause phlegm to gather in the body. This can sometimes stagnate and cause heat to rise, affecting the heart and resulting in angry outbursts, anxiety, agitation, or constipation.

'The kidneys are said to dominate reproduction in Chinese medicine. The kidneys are very much affected by overworking, which can lead to any number of issues directly relating to fertility, or indirectly to PMS. Kidney qi deficiency is one of the causes of liver qi stagnation. Kidneys and spleen work together to control water metabolism, if these two organs are not operating properly then water retention can occur.

'Acupuncture can release stagnation in meridians to allow the free flow of qi and blood, and maintain balance in the different organs which eases the emotional and physical symptoms of PMS. When the qi is flowing smoothly the hormone changes which take place after ovulation and before the period can be negotiated successfully.

'Depending on the individual diagnosis, specific advice might be given. For liver qi stagnation, vigorous exercise in the week before the period can be helpful. Women with spleen deficiency may need to eat warmer foods. If there are heart symptoms then meditation or tai chi is good. For women with kidney deficiency, more rest is highly recommended. In reality, a woman can present with a combination of imbalances, which can change according to what is going on in her life at the time. The beauty of Chinese medicine is in its adaptability to address symptoms as they move and change.'

Elaine Cook is an acupuncturist from the Dyke Road Natural Health Clinic in Brighton. She has over 20 years' experience working with women and fertility issues. To book an appointment with Elaine call the Dyke Road Clinic on 01273 561845 or visit Elaine's website www.ecacupuncture.co.uk

Finding an acupuncturist

The British Acupuncture Council (BAcC) is the largest body of professional acupuncturists in the UK, with over 3,000 registered traditional acupuncturists. They have an easy to use 'Practitioner Search' facility on their website which lists all the acupuncturists in your area. Visit www.acupuncture.org.uk to access this search facility.

Homeopathy

Homeopathy is based on the principle that you can treat 'like with like'; that is, a substance which causes symptoms when taken in large doses can be used in small amounts to treat those same symptoms. For example, drinking too much coffee can cause sleeplessness and agitation, so according to this principle, when made into the homeopathic remedy, Coffea, it could be used to treat people with these symptoms.

Homeopathic remedies

Homeopathic remedies are made by specialist homeopathic pharmacies using a technique known as 'dilution and succussion', which involves a specific form of vigorous shaking. Each remedy is made from plant, chemical, mineral or animal sources. The original material is diluted, then shaken vigorously (succussed). The number of times this is repeated determines the strength or 'potency' of the remedy.

As yet, science has been unable to explain the mechanism of action of these ultra-high dilutions in the body, but studies have demonstrated that homeopathically-prepared substances cause biological effects. One theory is that during the dilution and succussion process, an interaction between the original material and the water and alcohol it is mixed with occurs. This creates tiny new structures (nanostructures) which are the 'active ingredient' and remain present even when the sample has been diluted many, many times. There is also a growing body of evidence that homeopathic medicines have clinical effects.

Trusted brands

Although many homeopaths have the equipment needed to produce their own remedies, there are a number of well-known homeopathic pharmacies which you can purchase remedies from via their websites:

- Nelsons Homeopathy Pharmacy – www.nelsonsnaturalworld.com
- Helios Homeopathic Pharmacy – www.helios.co.uk
- Ainsworths Homeopathic Pharmacy – www.ainsworths.com

Many of these pharmacies have a homeopathic clinic that you can visit or telephone for advice. If you want to get a personalised homeopathic treatment plan then you'll need to book an appointment with a homeopath.

Susie talks to homeopath Lisa Bullen

Since making the move out of Brighton and settling into Barcombe, a beautiful countryside village in Sussex, I got to know homeopath Lisa Bullen. I asked Lisa to explain how homeopathy could be used to help PMS and here's what Lisa said:

'Homeopathy is a gentle, holistic method of healing, which concentrates on individual symptoms, both mental and physical. A woman's monthly cycle is the result of hormones working harmoniously in a complicated and sensitive endocrine system. Hormones can be easily affected by emotional shock, trauma or stress which may cause an imbalance, resulting in PMS or other menstrual disorders.

'Common PMS symptoms that homeopathy can really help with include swollen breasts, migraines, nausea, diarrhoea, bloating, constipation, altered libido, irritability, depression, indecision, panic attacks and, lastly, mood swings that can go from apathy to aggression.

'There are a number of well-known homeopathic remedies that can be bought over the counter, such as Sepia, Nux Vomica, Lachesis, Lycopodium and Chamomilla, which may offer relief, but it's always advisable to consult a professional homeopath if symptoms persist or if the improvement doesn't last.

'Here's a list of some recommended homeopathic remedies with the common mental and emotional PMS scenarios for which they can offer help:

- Nux Vomica – helpful for the female who literally loses the plot. She is unable to cope with her usual schedule and demands and will shout a lot and will have issues with "time" when her period is due, as just prior to her period she cannot sustain the pace. Physically she may have tender breasts, suffer with migraines, constipation and poor sleep.

- Sepia – helpful for the female who may assume a drudge mentality, too many demands are being made of her, she may feel stuck and she wants to get away. Sepia is a huge homeopathic hormonal remedy and as such covers a huge physical symptom picture including hot flushes, prolapses, irregular menses, morning sickness, to name a few.

- Lachesis – helpful for the female who will become insecure, suspicious and jealous. She will feel needy, and will feel markedly better once her period starts. She may have some physical symptoms of constriction which may be characterised by headaches and sore throats.

- Chamomilla – helpful for the female who becomes snappy, irritable and quarrelsome. She may be irritable and restless with the possible corresponding physical picture of lumbar back pain and an upset bowel.

- Lycopodium - helpful for the female who suffers irritability and indecision and she may feel cut off or distanced from her family. She may suffer bloating or flatulence and is likely to crave sugar and may have a marked aggravation time between 4pm and 8pm.

These are just a thumbnail of some of the homeopathic remedies that can be utilised to help with PMS. Each woman's physical, mental and emotional picture will lead to a bespoke homeopathic prescription for her.

Homeopath Lisa Bullen is based in East Sussex and can be contacted for information or appointments on Tel 01273 401100.

What to expect

A homeopath aims to get a thorough understanding of your health and the exact symptoms you are experiencing, so they can match a homeopathic remedy to you and your symptoms. You'll be asked questions about your current illness and other aspects of your health including your past medical history, diet, lifestyle and personality. The first consultation will take between one and two hours, follow-ups usually occur after four weeks and these sessions will be shorter.

Finding a homeopath

The Society of Homeopaths has a list of 'Registered Members' who may use the initials RSHom after their name. All of their members:

- Have satisfied the Society's educational and professional requirements.

- Practise in accordance with the Society's Code of Ethics and Practice and Core Criteria for Homeopathic Practice and National Occupational Standards for Homeopathy.

- Have full professional and indemnity insurance.

- Are responsible for continuing their personal and professional development

Visit www.homeopathy-soh.org to find a registered homeopath (search by postcode) or call the society on 0845 450 6611 for more information.

Aromatherapy

The practice of using aromatic oils to uplift the spirit and help cure diseases has been used by the world's greatest civilisations throughout history. Many texts from Asia to Ancient Egypt and much of the Mediterranean describe the various procedures and rituals involved in the making of healing ointments, medicated oils, poultices and healing perfumes.

Today, aromatherapy oils are pure essences extracted or distilled from plants. Flowers, leaves, roots, resins, seeds and fruits of many herbs, shrubs and trees are used to produce these aromatic oils, each with its own unique healing properties. Essential oils are absorbed into the body in two ways – through the skin (via massage or during bathing) and inhaled through the nose.

Therapeutic benefits

Some oils are used for their balancing effects on the nervous and hormonal systems and some for their ability to improve the function of bodily systems. Each essential oil has its own chemical identity, which produces unique properties. Essential oils can be antiseptic, analgesic, anti-inflammatory, anti-infectious and so on. They can be used to stimulate or sedate, and their powers to heal can be applied to physical, mental and emotional conditions.

Trusted brands

There are many companies all over the world that produce and sell essential oils and you can order oils for your own use at home from their websites. Or you'll find essential oils for sale in chemists, health food shops and natural health clinics. Good brands available in the UK include:

- NHR Organic Oils – www.nhrorganicoils.com

- New Directions – www.newdirectionsuk.com

- Tisserand Oils – www.tisserand.com

- Quinessence Aromatherapy – www.quinessence.com

You can use these oils in oil burners to scent a room or add a few drops of those known to help PMS to your bath. But the best way to truly benefit from the hormone-balancing effects of these special oils is to have a course of aromatherapy massage from a qualified aromatherapist.

Aromatherapy massage

Aromatherapy massage is a 20th century development pioneered by Marguerite Maury, an Austrian biochemist who combined the use of essential oils and body massage to create the aromatherapy massage treatment available today. She trained Micheline Arcier, who passed her knowledge on by training many of today's leading experts in the field of aromatherapy.

Aromatherapists are trained to choose essential oils for their specific properties. The skill is in selecting the most effective oil to treat your type of PMS, matching your symptoms to a unique combination of oils used during the massage. And it's not just the essential oils that you'll benefit from. Massage has been found in studies to reduce stress and anxiety, promote lymphatic flow and increase a sense of wellbeing.

Essential oils for PMS

PMS is a complex condition centered on hormone imbalance with accompanying physical, behavioural, mental and emotional symptoms. As you can imagine, there are a number of essential oils that can be used to address all these different symptoms. So getting advice from an aromatherapist as to which oils are best suited to your symptoms is highly recommended.

Susie talks to aromatherapist Laura Hoy

I spoke to Laura Hoy, aromatherapist and general manager at NHR Organic Oils to find out which oils she recommends for PMS. Here's what Laura said:

'Essential oils can be a powerful tool to support nurturing yourself throughout your cycle. It is important to be aware that your periods are a monthly cleansing, and if you experience difficult symptoms then this can reflect how you have been living, you could consider it your body's way of asking you to stop, slow down and take a look at what's been going on.

'You can use essential oils in different ways, for example in a bath blend (add 6-8 drops to a teaspoon of olive oil and add just before you get in), in a skin cream (available on request) or in a burner to scent a room. If you are using a burner, then prepare a space in the room for you to appreciate the oils, sit or lay for five minutes and just be with yourself.

'One of the most useful oils for PMS is geranium, as it balances the effects of hormones. This is a good oil to include in a regular ritual, for example in the bath or as a body moisturiser throughout your cycle. Rose is also extremely supportive in bringing stillness to the body. Gently massage a drop just under your collarbones, on both sides of your body, whenever you feel you need support.

'There are many symptoms associated with PMS and I tend to use specific essential oils to help ease individual symptoms. Here's my list of PMS recommendations:

- Skin problems: Palmarosa, benzoin, and lavender in a cream to apply on the affected area.

- Mood swings: Frankincense, myrrh and rose in a burner or bath blend.

- Poor sleep: Lavender, neroli and chamomile in a burner or bath blend before bed.

- Breast tenderness: Rose, lavender and myrrh in a skin cream or bath oil.

- Water retention: Lemon, geranium and lavender in a bath or skin cream.

- Anxiety: Peppermint in a burner

- Depleted, heavy, and feeling depressed: Melissa in a burner.

- Stressed, jittery, angst, racy: Rosemary in a burner.

- Muscle aches and pains: Rosemary and lavender in a skin cream or massage oil.

'However you choose to use essential oils, make sure your intention is to lovingly support yourself and truly heal rather than 'fix' the problem.'

For further advice or to request an essential oil blend you can contact Laura Hoy (Diploma in Aromatherapy and Essential Oil Science), Manager NHR Organic Oils by emailing laura@laurahoy.com or tel 07828954020.

What to expect

An aromatherapist will ask questions about your medical history, current ailments, personal stress, emotional issues, lifestyle and diet. Essential oils will be selected and blended with a carrier oil to be used during a full or partial body massage, designed to help support your health and wellbeing. A classic full body aromatherapy massage will include your back, arms, shoulders and neck, legs and the feet. Treatments last from 60-90 minutes for a full body massage.

Finding a therapist

The International Federation of Aromatherapists (IFA) holds a list of fully qualified aromatherapists who have the relevant insurance. You can search for a therapist using your postcode. Visit www.ifaroma.org for more info.

Flower essences

Flowers have been used in various ways for healing and mood enhancement throughout the ages. The concept of using a flower's energy for enhancing wellbeing, although less recognised, is ancient in origin and has been used by indigenous cultures for thousands of years. This method was used by Aborigines and was thought to have been employed in Egyptian times. In the 16th century, the physician Paracelsus was said to collect dew from flowers to treat his patients.

In more recent times, Dr. Edward Bach rediscovered flower essences in the early 1920s. In recognising the link between stress, emotions and illness, he believed that 'disease is in essence the result of a conflict between soul and mind and will never be eradicated except by spiritual and mental effort'. Bach gave up his profession as a Harley Street physician in order to search for a simple method of healing that embraced these principles – this resulted in the creation of the Bach Flower Remedies. His theories form the basis of our understanding today on how flower essences work and have provided the inspiration for the creation of many new ranges of flower essences.

Emotional healing

Flower essences provide a unique healing system which help individuals cope with the emotional challenges of life. Flower essences are tinctures of flowers and vibrations held in water and are self-adjusting, which means they energetically adapt themselves to the individual taking them.

Flower essence therapists believe that ill health is a physical manifestation of an emotional, psychological or spiritual imbalance. Flower essences work by supporting a person in such a way that they are able to process and clear their emotional issues so that healing and transformation can take place.

Flower essences and PMS

Flower essences can help you cope with the emotional challenges of major life events – divorce, moving home, changing jobs or becoming a parent. They can help you overcome shock and trauma and help you cope with fear, anxiety, phobia, guilt, grief, sadness and distress. There are many different flower essences available, each ready to support you through different emotional journeys. Since many of the symptoms of PMS have an emotional focus, flower essences can help you deal with the change in intensity of your emotions that you face each month.

Trusted brands

Dr. Bach pioneered the production of flower essences with his range of 38, essences and now there are companies all over the world that produce flower essences by varying methods and from different groups of flowers. Here's a list of the most wellknown brands that have many remedies to choose from:

- Bach Flower Remedies – www.bachcentre.com
- Australian Bush Flower Essences – www.ausflowers.com.au
- Findhorn Flower Essences – www.findhornessences.com
- Living Tree Orchid Essences – www.healingorchids.com

You use these essences by taking them under the tongue, rubbing them on pulse points, placing them on the meridians and chakras, adding them to a bath or simply spraying them in the air or around the body. These gentle remedies can have powerful effects, so it's well worth discussing your PMS symptoms with a qualified therapist who can then select an appropriate combination of essences for you.

What to expect

A flower essence therapist aims to get a thorough understanding of your emotional, psychological and spiritual health. You'll be asked to talk about the emotions that you experience and reflect on how these impact on your day-to-day life and relationships. Your therapist will suggest various flower essences to help you overcome these emotional imbalances.

Find a therapist

The British Flower and Vibrational Essences Association (BFVEA) hold a list of fully qualified therapists who have relevant insurance. The members' list is split into two categories.

1. Practitioner Members – therapists who have completed a flower essence course that is not BFVEA compliant but which meets BFVEA minimum standards.

2. Advanced Practitioner Members – therapists who have completed a BFVEA compliant course.

Visit www.bfvea.com to search for a registered flower essence therapist according to your postcode.

Natural hormone therapy

Natural hormone therapy is gaining popularity by women who need to take hormones to help ease their PMS but who don't want to resort to synthetic hormones due to their associated health risks.

Oestrogen and progesterone have quite different and opposing roles within the body. Oestrogen often stimulates body cells, whereas progesterone tends to have more of a calming effect. If oestrogen becomes too high in relation to progesterone (known as 'oestrogen dominance') then you can start to experience a number of unbearable premenstrual symptoms.

Protective progesterone

Over the fertile lifespan, a woman who is exposed to more progesterone than oestrogen is likely to reach menopause in a healthier state, with less risk of reproductive tissue cancers, osteoporosis, obesity or diabetes. Pregnancy is a time in a woman's life when the cycle is put on hold and progesterone becomes abundant. In the past, a woman in her fertile years would have children young, and more of them, than is currently the case. This confers a 'progesterone positive' state, which is largely beneficial for female health.

Oestrogen trend

In our current society, we have fewer children and later in life. This means our bodies are exposed to the cycle of oestrogen and progesterone many more times over the fertile years. We are more exposed to our own oestrogen than is perhaps good for us, since we don't take the 'rest' of pregnancy often enough. We are also exposed to xenoestrogens in our food chain and our diets contain more sugar, refined carbohydrates, saturated fat, salt and alcohol with little fibre, all of which encourages oestrogen to become too high and progesterone too low. It's no wonder the 'women of today' are experiencing PMS.

Health risks of synthetic hormones

Although many doctors have started to recommend self-help strategies such as diet and lifestyle changes as a way to deal with PMS, many women, of all ages, resort to prescriptions of synthetic hormones to find relief from their hormonal symptoms.

At first glance this seems harmless enough, but a closer look reveals that these synthetic hormones are prone to causing havoc with the natural functioning of the human body. They are designed to bind with cells, but do not necessarily effect the same intensity of changes within a cell. It's a bit like a key that fits a lock but instead of turning it once, it turns it over and over and over again. The health risks associated with taking synthetic hormones have now been very well documented. Increased risk of breast, ovarian and endometrial cancers, increased risk of stroke and cardiovascular disease along with a prolonged and challenging menopause are but a few.

Natural hormones

Natural hormones are available but not readily prescribed, and in this country the only commonly-used form is a progesterone suppository, which can be administered vaginally or rectally. Oestrogen and progesterone are both available in natural forms as creams and capsules from European pharmacies, and there are several natural progesterone creams available online.

Natural hormone therapy and PMS

There are a number of doctors in the UK who will privately prescribe natural oestrogen and progesterone capsules with good results for PMS. Of course, the benefit of using natural hormones is that they have the same chemical structure as the hormones that your body produces. This means they cause the same effect on cells as your own hormones do, so you get all of the benefits and none of the risks. Sometimes these hormones are referred to as bio-identical.

Susie talks to Dr Lisa McCready

I spoke to Dr Lisa McCready, who has been prescribing natural hormones in her female health clinic for several years, to find out how natural hormone therapy can help women with PMS. Here's what Dr McCready had to say:

'Taking natural hormones can certainly help to reduce PMS symptoms and severity, but making changes to your diet and lifestyle can help your body regain its own ability to maintain hormone balance.

'Oestrogen dominance, a state of affairs where for multiple reasons women are overexposed to the harmful effects of too much natural and synthetic oestrogen whilst lacking adequate protective progesterone, is a key trigger for PMS. Taking natural progesterone, in capsule form – at the right time in the cycle and at the right dose – is a very effective way to correct oestrogen dominance and ease PMS.'

Dr Lisa McCready is an NHS Consultant with an interest in natural medicine. Her main area of expertise is women's health and she prescribes natural hormones for a range of conditions including PMS, menopausal symptoms, migraine, recurrent miscarriage and infertility. Contact Dr McCready on lisamccready@mac.com.

Expert advice

As Dr McCready points out here, it's the dose and time in your cycle that is important and this is what a private doctor will be able to oversee. Yes you can buy natural progesterone creams over the Internet, but it's not advisable to experiment with these on your own. It's the capsules that are much more effective, as you have better control over your timings and dosages with capsules than you do with a cream. So be smart and take advice from a doctor.

Finding a doctor

Doctors that prescribe natural hormones in capsule form are hard to track down. One tip is to contact a German company called 'Receptura', who manufacture and distribute natural hormones to doctors. They are very helpful and can let you know if they have any doctors registered with them in your area. Receptura – www.receptura.de, tel: +49 (0) 69 92 880-300, email: info@ receptura.de.

Summing Up

▪ As you can see, there are lots of different types of natural therapies and remedies that you can use to help you achieve and maintain hormone balance and get your PMS under control.

▪ Take your time and consider which one feels the best or more suited to you.

▪ Next, contact at least three therapists and talk to them over the phone so that you can choose the one that you feel the most comfortable with. This way you will get the most benefit from your appointments.

Chapter Nine

Stress and PMS

Stress undoubtedly has a big influence on PMS, and the more stressed you are the worse your PMS is likely to be. Stress has many different guises and two of the most popular forms of stress for PMS include relationship stress and stress from a busy, overcommitted schedule. The good thing about PMS is that it happens at around the same time of the month, every month, which means you can plan ahead. But many women fail to keep their schedule light during their premenstrual week so they end up overwhelmed and overemotional.

Superwoman syndrome

It seems that many 21st century women are running around like headless chickens trying to keep up with the stresses and strains of modern life – having a successful career, raising a family, keeping a tidy home, enjoying a full social life, being a culinary genius, maintaining a fulfilling relationship, keeping trim and fit and maintaining youthful looks. No wonder women are so frazzled! No wonder we are suffering from fertility issues and stress-related disorders, and no wonder PMS is so prominent in our society today.

It's time for women to realise that they are not and should not feel they have to be superhuman! You see, for 7-10 days out of every month your hormones fluctuate in such a way that it's impossible for your body to physically, psychologically and emotionally cope with the extremely stressful demands of day-to-day living. All it takes is a little bit of planning ahead and you will be much more able to cope with your PMS.

'You see, for 7-10 days out of every month your hormones fluctuate in such a way that it's impossible for your body to physically, psychologically and emotionally cope with the extremely stressful demands of day-to-day living.'

Making changes

- Take a good look at your life and see if you are suffering from 'superwoman syndrome'.

- Stop putting such pressure on yourself to achieve in so many areas of your life.

- Think about dropping the activities that you don't enjoy anymore.

- Have you, over time, taken on more and more commitments and now actually feel overcommitted? Take steps to offload some commitments so you are back to a schedule that feels more manageable.

- Are you now in a situation where you can afford to get some help at home? You could get someone to do the cleaning, ironing, book keeping or even someone to cook freezer meals or do school drop off and/or pick up.

Clear your diary

Every month your PMS hits around the same time. Your anxiety notches up a gear, your energy takes a nosedive, you know you're going to experience a headache at some point and it's almost guaranteed that someone – be it a shop keeper, a call centre telephone operator, one of your children, your partner or even one of your parents – is going to get snapped at or shouted at. You'll then spend a few days feeling guilty and giving yourself a hard time about how emotional and poorly behaved you have been!

If this is a good description of how your premenstrual week goes every month, then it's time to realise that during your premenstrual week you need to lighten your load. Clear your diary of unnecessary events and keep it clear so that you can put your feet up. This will have a phenomenal impact on your PMS.

Making changes

- Go through your diary and mark with a highlighter the week, each month, that is likely to be your premenstrual week.

- Be very strict about what you take on during this week. If friends and family are planning social events then see if you can suggest dates that fall outside of your highlighted zone.

- If you have any scope at work to create a lighter workload during these highlighted weeks, then start to filter your work in this way.

- If your children want to organise play dates then use your highlighted weeks as good weeks for them to go to their friends' houses and suggest days outside of your highlighted zones as good days for you to host play dates.

- If you still want to be social then instead of planning nights out during your highlighted weeks, plan nights in – get your girlfriends over for a movie night or plan a 'takeaway' night in with your partner so you don't have to cook.

- Make an absolute commitment to keep these weeks as clear as possible, you will be very thankful for this lighter schedule and this will help you feel less overwhelmed.

Ask for support

Your PMS doesn't just affect you! It also affects everyone around you – your partner, your family, your friends, your work colleagues and anyone else that gets in your way! It's perfectly clear to everyone around you that you are having a hard time coping – physically and emotionally – but how prepared are you to admit this to yourself? There's nothing more irritating than hearing your partner say 'you're overreacting, it's your time of month' and the most irritating part of this, is the fact that he's right!

Some men are very sensitive and understanding and will naturally take on a much more supportive role as the warning signs that PMS is brewing start to be revealed. He might offer to cook dinner, help out more with the kids and give you the space and relaxation time that you need for your body to cope with the hormonal changes that you are experiencing.

Other partners might have developed a coping strategy of keeping quiet and keeping out of the way. But clearly you need more support and if your partner doesn't understand how to offer this up then it's up to you to guide him with suggestions of what you need.

Some women don't find it easy to ask for help as they see it as a sign of weakness or because they feel they don't want people to know they can't cope. It's normal to need help and support at this time and asking for it can often bring you closer together and make your friendships stronger.

Making changes

- Explain to your partner how your PMS makes you feel. Let him know that during your premenstrual phase you need some help and support.

- Be very specific about the type of help and support that you need. Your partner can't read your mind!

  - Would you like him to give you a bit of space so you can be on your own?

  - Would you like him to be more helpful around the home? Be specific – cooking, washing-up, tidying up . . .

  - Do you need him to get the kids to bed?

  - Do you want a bit of peace and quiet?

  - Would you rather that he went over to his friends' houses rather than them coming over to your house?

  - Would you like him to do the weekly shop?

  - Would you like him to organise a takeaway and a movie?

- Work out what works best for you as a couple, go through a list of good ideas for support and ask him which ones he feels he could do . . .

- If you have a particularly bad month of PMS then who, other than your partner, could you call on for support – close friends, Mum, sister?

Relationship issues

During non-premenstrual weeks you have the ability to tolerate the things about your relationship that you feel aren't quite right. However, during your premenstrual week changes in your hormones trigger your brain chemistry to

'It's normal to need help and support at this time and asking for it can often bring you closer together and make your friendships stronger.'

be altered in a such a way that you become much more sensitive to and much less able to tolerate the issues that exist within your relationship. As you tip more into your premenstrual hormone imbalance, your mood becomes more unpredictable and eventually you blow your fuse.

At this point you are unlikely to hold back and you'll deliver to your partner a detailed account in great fury expressing all the things that aren't right in your relationship and whilst you're at it you'll add in a few extra issues just for good measure! Whilst you might feel better for having a good rant, your partner might be left feeling demoralised and unappreciated.

There's also the fact that your partner may feel like he has a free pass to ignore the issues that you have raised because you just behaved in such an inappropriate and extreme way. If this is a pattern that is being repeated every month then clearly the issues that you are ranting about do need to be addressed. Schedule some time during the better half of your cycle when you can talk openly with each other about these issues, offering up possible solutions and being equally prepared to listen to each other and to action positive changes. And if you are unable to resolve these issues by yourselves, then be prepared to book a course of relationship counselling.

Making changes

- During a non-PMS week make a list of the issues you feel make your relationship challenging.

- Explain to your partner that during your premenstrual phase you find certain aspects of your relationship more challenging than when you are not suffering from PMS.

- Find time to talk about the issues that you have concerns about and together work out ways to resolve them.

- Consider joint relationship counselling if you both feel you would benefit.

Susie talks to life coach Mark Shields

Since so many of us find it hard to ask for support and keep our schedules light, I talked to Mark Shields, Life Coach and Managing Director of Life Practice UK, who uses a Five Stage Plan for PMS which involves – Strategy, Acceptance, Diet and Exercise, Time out and Communication. We've already heard about how diet and exercise can help PMS but I asked Mark about his other stages, here's what he said:

'I suggest my clients should approach their PMS in the following way . . .

- Strategy – The feelings experienced during PMS mean that things which aren't usually a problem can be magnified by ten, often leaving you overwhelmed and stressed. The moment you identify this as "normal" for this week of the month you also develop a strategy to combat these feelings and emotions.

- Acceptance – Acceptance is a positive emotion and can change the direction your emotions are heading in. By accepting how you feel you are able to be objective and think clearly. Fighting emotions and feelings will only create internal conflict and generate more negative emotions which can spiral your feelings downwards.

- Time out – It's important to ensure that you have some "time for yourself". Take thirty minutes each day, put your favourite relaxing music on or use meditation or self-relaxing breathing techniques. This will strengthen your mental state and ability to cope.

- Communication – Although you are experiencing all sorts of challenging emotions this week, remember if you don't tell anyone, they won't know and may add fuel to the fire. Tell your husband or partner how you feel and ask for some help and understanding. Explain to your children that Mummy needs extra help this week. People will understand if you communicate and ask for some understanding.

'By incorporating these four factors alongside better diet and improved exercise you can start to see your PMS improve.'

Mark Shields, life coach, author, media expert and motivational speaker, is Managing Director of Life Practice UK, Specialists in Personal and Business Coaching. Contact: 01462 451473, www.lifepractice.co.uk, info@lifepractice.co.uk.

Action plan

※ Reduce the amount of pressure you are under – at home, at work and in your social network during your premenstrual weeks.

※ Call on support from your partner, family and friends. Be specific about the type of support you need each month.

※ Plan ahead by highlighting your premenstrual weeks in the months ahead in your diary.

※ Be committed to keeping these premenstrual weeks as clear as possible so you can take adequate rest.

※ Find ways to address any recurring issues you have in your relationship.

※ Improve your communication between you and your partner, family and close friends so you can call on them for support when you need to.

Summing Up

- It's perfectly normal when you are in your premenstrual week to feel like you are unable to cope.

- Make life easy for yourself by keeping your schedule light during these times and leaning on your partner, family and friends for support. This might feel a little uncomfortable to start with, but your whole family will thank you for starting to deal with your PMS in this way!

- Time out and relaxation is very important so make sure you make this a priority.

Chapter Ten

Seven Steps to Beating PMS

Step 1 – Chart your symptoms

PMS symptoms occur during the two weeks prior to your period and there are a number of symptoms that you could be experiencing. Your symptoms can change from one month to another and you'll also find that some months your symptoms can be very extreme and other months very mild. This is because your ability to achieve perfect hormone balance every month is challenged by a number of dietary and lifestyle factors.

For example, you might have already noticed that your premenstrual symptoms of irritability and mood swings are much more extreme after a month of increased stress at work or at home. Similarly, a month with fuller social commitments and considerably higher alcohol consumption may trigger your premenstrual sugar cravings to become much more uncontrollable.

Charting your symptoms

PMS only occurs for a few days out of every month and for the rest of the time you feel pretty much like 'you'. Once your period begins you're back to feeling more like yourself again making it hard to remember how many types of symptoms you experienced and the intensity of each of these symptoms. This is why charting your symptoms is so important. By recording what you feel and how intensely you feel it – on the actual day that you are feeling it – you can start to build an accurate picture of your particular type of PMS.

Monitoring progress

Another factor to take into consideration is that your road to recovery from PMS may take several months, or even a year if you have extremely severe PMS. Some women are able to make all of the necessary dietary changes, increase their exercise, take a handful of natural remedies, have a course of acupuncture and make radical changes to their schedule and lifestyle to reduce their stress and toxicity all within the time frame of just one to three months. These women are likely to have eased their symptoms within just a few menstrual cycles.

However, many women would find making so many changes unrealistic and actually very stressful. It's very important that you 'go at your own pace' making the changes each month that you feel you can easily accommodate and achieve. This will slow progress down but at least you won't be stressed and you are much more likely to maintain the changes that you have put in place. The outcome of being free from PMS is the same, it's just that the journey takes a little longer.

Boosting motivation

Charting your symptoms each month can be a great motivational tool and many women find that it actually helps them 'stay on track' rather than sabotage their progress if they hit particularly challenging months. For instance, eight months into your programme you might feel particularly low and tell yourself there's no point avoiding chocolate as you feel your PMS is the same as it was before you started changing your diet. If you haven't been recording your symptoms then you'll have no evidence to prove or disprove your theory, you'll give into your urges and sabotage your progress.

But if you have been charting your symptoms for the last eight cycles and you can see that your mood swings have gone down from a high 10/10 to a much improved 4/10 then it's pretty clear that avoiding chocolate has been helping. This can give you the strength, determination and motivation to stay off the chocolate rather than cave into your cravings.

Action plan

Use the Monthly PMS Symptom Chart in chapter 3 to record your symptoms each month, the benefits of charting it are:

- Creates a clear picture of your core symptoms and your accessory symptoms each month.

- Helps you track the intensity of your symptoms each month so you can monitor your progress.

- Acts as a motivational tool helping you stay on track.

- Helps indicate which factors trigger which symptoms, when you add details of the type of month you've had, (diet, stress etc.)..

Step 2 – Identify your PMS profile

The early chapters of this book are a bit of a biology lesson but they help you grasp an understanding of the glands and hormones involved in your 28-day cycle. PMS is simply a sign that somewhere along the way your body has strayed from the ideal balance of hormones that's needed for your menstrual cycle to function normally.

PMS profiles and hormones

Back in the 1980s, Dr Abraham noticed that women with the same type of hormone imbalance suffered PMS with the same group of symptoms. His work was groundbreaking and he was the first person to categorise PMS into different hormone and symptom profile groups:

- PMS-A – Too much oestrogen, or too much oestrogen and not enough progesterone.

- PMS-C – Too much insulin.

- PMS-H – Too much aldosterone.

- PMS-D – Too little oestrogen, too much progesterone, too much testosterone.

- PMDD – A more extreme and debilitating version of PMS-D.

PMS profiles and treatment

All the PMS profiles respond well to the general dietary and lifestyle advice that's recommended throughout this book. But research over the last few decades has revealed that the different PMS profiles also benefit from a few specific dietary recommendations, supplements, herbal extracts and natural remedies.

- PMS-A – Diet high in phytoestrogens, plus soy-isoflavones, zinc, Agnus castus.

- PMS-C – GI diet, plus chromium, magnesium, cinnamon.

- PMS-H – Low salt diet, plus magnesium, liquorice extract, GLA, vitamin E.

- PMS-D – Diet rich in tryptophan, plus 5-HTP, St John's wort.

- PMDD - Prescription anti-depression medications.

Action plan

Use the PMS Profile Questionnaire in chapter 4 to calculate your PMS profile. It's not unusual to have more than one profile. The benefits of knowing your PMS profile include:

- Insight into which hormones are out of balance.

- Information as to the types of foods and nutrients to include in your diet.

- Information as to the natural remedies and nutritional supplements that are best suited to your type of PMS.

Step 3 – Reduce your stress

Without a doubt, stress has a big impact on PMS as it has the ability to turn up the severity of your symptoms each month. Throughout your life you are exposed to many different sources of stress. If you want to be free from PMS then you need to start making changes so you can be free from stress!

Different forms of stress

* Performance-related stress at school or college.

* Stressful family dynamics.

* Emotional stress from interpersonal relationships.

* Stress in the work place.

* Stress from a major life event such as moving house, getting married, starting a new job.

* Stress from shock or trauma, for example death of a loved one, being in an accident, going through separation or divorce.

* Simply stress from being too busy, not being able to say 'no' and ending up overwhelmed by family, work and social commitments.

Stress and PMS

So why does stress have such a big impact on PMS? Well when you are stressed you produce more of the stress hormone cortisol. Cortisol hitches a ride around your body on the transport protein that also carries progesterone. This transport protein is called cortisol-binding globulin, or CBG for short. During times of stress, CBG tells progesterone to wait in line whilst it deals with cortisol. The longer you remain stressed the longer progesterone waits in line and the more imbalanced your hormones become.

As you reduce your level of stress, so your cortisol levels drop and progesterone gets to hitch a ride on CBG again. Oestrogen and progesterone become more balanced and your PMS starts to melt away.

Action plan

* Take time to sit down with a notebook and write down all the areas of your life that you feel you are exposed to stress. Think of ways or solutions that you can try that will help to dissipate these forms of stress.

- Learn to say 'no'! Always check in with yourself before committing to yet another social or family commitment.

- Use the support that you have around you. When you do start to feel overwhelmed call on the support of your partner, friends and family. You don't have to go it alone.

- Delegate – if you can find someone to delegate your workload to when you are feeling stretched, then go for it!

- Talk things through. If your stress comes from your interpersonal relationships, then it's time to start talking. Share your concerns and worries with those concerned, voice your feelings and consider counselling to help heal unresolved issues.

- Communicate! Finding ways to improve your communication in all areas of your life – family, work, friends – can be of great benefit. Better communication helps to strengthen friendships, nurture support and ease stress.

Step 4 – Improve your diet

There is lots of scientific research to indicate that a diet high in saturated fat, sugar, salt, alcohol and low in fibre and good fats increases your risk of PMS. Eating too many of the wrong foods – red meat, dairy products, refined carbohydrates, sugar and alcohol can cause oestrogen and progesterone to become out of balance. And eating too much salt has been shown to increase water retention and breast tenderness.

Taking the time to look at what you are eating is a very necessary step if you want your PMS to improve. What you eat shapes your hormone picture each month. So cut out the foods that are known to contribute to PMS and start to follow the advice for a hormone-balancing diet.

Foods to reduce:

- Sugar, refined carbohydrates and fizzy/diet drinks.
- Salt.

- Red meat and dairy products (milk, cheese, cream, butter).
- Processed foods, ready meals, junk food and fried food.
- Caffeine.
- Alcohol.

Hormone-balancing diet

- Drink plenty of water and cut back on caffeine by swapping tea and coffee for herbal alternatives.
- Aim for the majority of your diet to be made up from fresh natural foods.
- Follow the principles of the low GI and GL diet discussed in chapter 7, this improves fibre intake and boosts complex carbohydrates needed for better blood sugar and hormone balance.
- Eat oily fish at least 3-4 times a week.
- Include more vegetarian meals into your weekly meal planning.
- Include foods rich in zinc, magnesium and vitamin B6 and E and add in foods that contain hormone balancing phytoestrogens.
- Find lots of healthy snacks to enjoy as this will help keep you on track. Fresh fruits, vegetable crudities and nuts and seeds are good options.

Action plan

- Get organised! Changing your diet means that you need to shop for different foods and cook different meals.
- Visit your local health food shop as they will have lots of the nuts, seeds, wholegrains and complex carbohydrates you'll need. Sign up for a local Organic Veg Box Scheme.
- Take your time. You don't have to make all of the changes at once. Change a couple of things each week; this will be much more manageable and less stressful.

※ Get a few new cook books as these are a great source of inspiration when it comes to meal planning. A GI cookbook is a good idea, as are a fish and vegetarian cookbook.

Step 5 – Reduce your toxicity

Your liver has a big part to play in your ability to maintain hormone balance, so keeping this organ in tip-top condition is important if you want to see improvements in your PMS. One of the main jobs of your liver is to constantly filter out toxins and waste products from your bloodstream and process them for elimination from your body.

Body toxicity and PMS

There are certain lifestyle factors such as smoking, drinking too much alcohol and taking social drugs that cause your liver to become preoccupied with 'body cleansing' to such a degree that hormone balance gets forgotten. Eating too much saturated fat and processed food can also cause your liver to become sluggish and 'clogged up' making hormone balance a tricky business.

Liver support

The good news is that if you cut back on your toxic load then your liver will respond accordingly. If your liver is very congested and tired due to years of overindulgence, then there are lots of foods, supplements and herbal remedies that can help to cleanse and regenerate your liver:

※ Foods – celery, garlic, leeks, chicory, endive.

※ Spices – turmeric, chilli.

※ Supplements – B-vitamins, inositol, choline, methionine, glutathione, MSM and antioxidants.

※ Herbal remedies – milk thistle, dandelion extract, artichoke extract.

Action plan

▓ Reduce alcohol to three glasses of wine a week – one glass on three separate days. If this level is unachievable then aim for the guidelines of 14 units a week. Spread these units across the week and have at least three alcohol-free days a week. If reducing down to 14 units is hard to achieve then talk to your doctor about getting help.

▓ If you want to give up smoking then there are plenty of support groups to contact and your GP can point you in the right direction for support.

▓ If you regularly use social drugs then these could be impacting on your hormone balance. Take steps to cut back and find support if you need additional help.

▓ Include foods in your diet that help to support and cleanse your liver and take a 1-3 month course of supplements or herbal extracts to help replenish and recharge your liver. It's best to do this under the guidance of a Nutritional Therapist.

Step 6 – Increase your exercise

We've all got the message that exercise is good for us but many of us still find it hard, for one reason or another, to fit it into our daily or weekly routine. I can't stress enough how important cardiovascular exercise is for hormone balance. Exercise helps to improve your fitness, your body condition and your body shape. All key factors if you want to look and feel fantastic! But aside from sorting out your general fitness and body issues exercise has a direct impact on your hormones.

Exercise and PMS

▓ The more active you are in your day-to-day life, the more chance you have of maintaining good hormone balance. If you drive to work, sit at a desk all day, eat lunch at your desk, drive home and then sit in front of the TV all evening then your level of fitness will be pretty poor. This is a very sedentary lifestyle and living this way causes your body to stagnate and this will be reflected in your mood, body condition and your level of PMS.

- Cardiovascular exercise helps to promote a healthy BMI and reduce excess body fat which means that your fat cells produce less of the extra oestrogen that can lead to hormone imbalance.

- Exercise helps encourage a better balance of brain chemicals (neurotransmitters) that control your emotions. This means your emotions will be more stable during your premenstrual phase.

- Exercise encourages your liver to produce the transport proteins that carry oestrogen and progesterone around your body, improving hormone balance.

Action plan

- Ditch the excuses – it's time to get active!

- Find something that you enjoy, there are so many different types of activities and exercise classes that you can get involved with.

- If you are very unfit then start to regain your fitness by going on a 30-minute walk a day, picking up the pace as your fitness increases.

- Aim to include at least 30-60 minutes of cardiovascular exercise three times a week.

- Team up with an exercise buddy if you feel you are lacking in motivation.

- Join a gym and have a session with a Personal Trainer so you can get an appropriate exercise plan formulated for your level of fitness.

Step 7 – Natural therapies and remedies

Once you have put steps 1-6 into practice, then your body is set up to get hormone balance back on track. The more effort you put in, the quicker you'll see results. But if your progress isn't as quick as you'd liked or if it's been difficult to make adequate changes, then you will benefit from some additional help.

There are a phenomenal number of natural therapies to choose from. Some of these are very 'new age' and not suited to everyone, whilst others have become very mainstream and widely accepted by our modern day society. So find a therapy that you feel will work for you. The therapies that I have talked about in chapter 8 are the ones that I have found work well with nutritional therapy and tend to get good results for PMS. When choosing a natural therapy or remedy there are three important things to consider:

- Always get advice from an appropriately qualified professional when selecting remedies like nutritional supplements, herbs, flower essences, homeopathic remedies, aromatherapy oils and other healing remedies. Don't self-medicate as this can be dangerous.

- If you are taking any prescription medications then check with your doctor that the suggested remedies are suitable to take alongside your medication.

- If you are going to book a course of natural therapy then firstly find a therapist that has a good reputation, adequate qualifications and is a member of a professional association. Secondly, choose someone that you feel comfortable with, this is particularly important if you have emotional issues to be addressed.

Natural therapies for PMS

- Nutritional therapy.

- Acupuncture.

- Homeopathy.

- Aromatherapy.

- Flower remedies.

- Natural hormone therapy.

Summing Up

■ Think about which natural therapy would best suit you.

■ Go onto the website for the professional organisation associated with that therapy and use the 'find a therapist in your area' search. Contact at least three therapists in your area and chat with them over the phone, then book with the therapist you feel the most comfortable with.

■ Most natural therapies don't work overnight so although one appointment will be helpful and insightful, your body will benefit much more from a course of appointments. Your therapist will be able to advise you as to how many appointments you are likely to need.

■ Fully commit to the appointments and to the advice that you are given during your appointments. This way you'll get good results that will have long-lasting effects on your PMS.

Chapter Eleven

Recipes

There are so many healthy foods that are packed full of all the nutrients your body needs to maintain hormone balance. Focusing on reducing foods containing saturated fat, sugar, salt and starch is just one part of getting your diet right. You also need to learn how to incorporate all of the 'healthy hormone' foods that have been mentioned in previous chapters if you want to lessen your symptoms of PMS.

If you are already a good cook and happy to get creative in the kitchen, then you'll be very comfortable coming up with your own recipes and ideas that incorporate the 'healthy hormone' foods listed in chapter 7. However, if you're not a keen cook or don't feel very confident in the kitchen, then you might feel like you don't know where to start. To help you get started I showed the list of 'healthy hormone' foods to Claudine Allen, private chef and founder of Moreish Bespoke Catering and asked her to come up with some recipes that were simple and easy to follow. Here are her delicious suggestions, there's one recipe for each of the specific nutrients so you can easily top-up on whichever nutrients you feel you need to help clear your PMS.

Vitamin E boost

Foods rich in vitamin E include fish, sunflower seeds, avocado, mango, almonds, hazelnuts and green vegetables. Try this great fish and mango salsa recipe for a quick vitamin E boost.

Oily fish with mango salsa

Serves 4

Ingredients

600g fresh sardines

For the salsa

1 pink grapefruit, peeled, segmented and chopped

1 ripe mango, peeled and chopped

1 ripe avocado, quartered

½ red onion

Large handful mint

1 red chilli, seeded and finely chopped (optional)

½ tbsp red wine vinegar

1½ tbsp sunflower oil

Salt and black pepper

Method

To make the salsa you need to combine the grapefruit, mango, red onion, chilli and mint with the vinegar and oil in a bowl. Next cut each avocado quarter into fine slices and gently add to salsa. Add salt and pepper to taste. Next, brush sardines with a little olive oil and grill on a high heat for about 8-10 minutes, until just cooked through. Divide the sardines between four plates, adding a spoonful of salsa to each plate and serve with a green salad.

Vitamin B6 boost

Foods rich in vitamin B6 include milk, lean meats, banana, pulses, brown rice and prunes. Try this delicious smoothie for a quick vitamin B6 boost.

Banana and prune smoothie

Serves 2

Ingredients

250ml semi-skimmed milk

1 medium banana

50g prunes (4 or 5), roughly chopped

Method

Place all the ingredients into a blender and pulse until smooth. Divide into glasses and serve.

Zinc boost

Good food sources of zinc include oysters, lean meats, fish, pumpkin seeds, peanuts and split peas. Try this great chicken curry recipe to top up on zinc.

Chicken and peanut curry

Serves 4

Ingredients

2 tbsp peanut or olive oil

2 large boneless, skinless chicken breasts, chopped into bite-sized pieces (about 550g)

1 large onion, sliced

2 garlic cloves

100g unsalted peanuts, roughly chopped (hulled or skin on)

2 tbsp red Thai curry paste

1 butternut squash (about 500g) peeled, deseeded and cut into chunks

400ml reduced fat coconut milk

200ml hot water

Large handful coriander

Method

In a large pan heat the oil and sauté the onions until they are just beginning to brown, then add the Thai paste and garlic and cook for a further minute stirring continually. Next add the peanuts and continue to cook for a further minute, stirring so that mixture does not stick. Then stir in the chicken pieces and squash, coating the pieces with the peanut mixture. Add the coconut milk and water and bring to the boil then reduce heat and simmer for 20-25 minutes or until the chicken is cooked through and the squash is tender. Garnish with roughly chopped coriander leaves before serving. Serve with brown basmati rice.

Magnesium boost

Foods rich in magnesium include green leafy vegetables, buckwheat, figs, almonds and cashews. This buckwheat pancake recipe is a great breakfast treat and a good way to increase your magnesium intake.

Buckwheat pancakes with figs

Ingredients

For the batter

70g buckwheat flour

1 tsp baking powder

1 medium-sized egg

250ml semi-skimmed milk

Sunflower oil for frying

4 drops liquid stevia

1 tsp cinnamon

For the filling

12 figs

6 drops stevia liquid

2 slices of orange

Water for cooking

2 tbsp cashew nuts

Method

Start by making the stewed fig filling. Add the figs, stevia and orange slices to a small pan and add enough water to just cover them. Bring to the boil and then reduce heat to a gentle simmer for 35 minutes, stirring occasionally, so the figs stew down into a nice compote consistency. Make the batter mix by adding all the batter ingredients to a blender and pulse until smooth. Set aside and leave to stand for 10 minutes. Pour a small amount of oil in a frying pan and heat, then pour about an eighth of the mixture (roughly about one and a half tablespoons) into the pan to make a small saucer-sized pancake. Cook until brown and then flip and brown the other side. Remove from the pan and keep warm whist cooking the rest of the pancakes. Place two pancakes onto each plate, drizzle with the stewed fig mixture and top with a sprinkling of cashew nuts and serve.

Omega-3 boost

Oily fish are one of the best sources of omega-3 fats and this includes salmon, trout, mackerel, herring, fresh tuna, sardines and pilchards. Eating these fish regularly can help to boost your omega-3 status. Try this salmon salad to get you started.

Salmon and fennel salad

Serves 4

Ingredients

4 small salmon fillets

120g bag watercress, spinach and rocket salad

1 fennel bulb, thinly sliced

410g can borlotti beans, drained

100ml natural yoghurt

Zest and juice of 1 orange

1 tsp lemon juice

Small handful dill, roughly chopped

Salt and pepper

Method

Steam the salmon fillets for 8-10 minutes or until just cooked. Peel and discard the skin and flake the salmon into large chunks. Mix together the salad leaves, fennel and beans and arrange on a serving dish. Next mix 2 tbsp of orange juice, orange zest and the lemon juice with the yoghurt and season this with salt and pepper to taste. Scatter the flaked salmon pieces and dill over the salad and drizzle with the yoghurt dressing. Serve.

Indoles boost

Indoles occur naturally in cruciferous vegetables and help with hormone balance. Here's a great soup recipe for a quick indoles boost.

Broccoli soup

Serves 4

Ingredients

600g broccoli, broken up into florets and stalks chopped

1tbsp olive oil

1 large onion, chopped

1 medium potato, chopped into small cubes

1.2 litres boiling water

Handful walnuts, chopped

Method

Heat the oil in a pan and add the onion and cook on medium heat until soft but not coloured, this should take about five minutes. Next add the potato and cook for further two minutes then add the broccoli and pour in the water and boil for 5-7 minutes or until the broccoli is soft but still bright green. Allow to cool slightly before either transferring to blender and pulsing until smooth or using a hand blender to do the same. Re-heat until hot but not quite boiling. Serve sprinkled with chopped walnuts.

Phytoestrogen boost

Foods rich in natural phytoestrogens include soya beans, soya milk, edamame beans, soya yoghurt, miso, tempeh, soya sauce, flaxseeds, sesame seeds, sunflower seeds, almonds, chestnuts, peanuts and mung beans. Try this healthy miso soup for a quick phytoestrogen boost. For fresh miso paste visit www.miso.co.uk.

Miso soup

Serves 4

Ingredients

200g silken tofu, cubed

1 litre organic chicken or vegetable stock

2 tbsp fresh miso paste

1 tbsp mirin

1 tbsp sunflower oil

1tbsp light soya sauce

2 spring onions, finely sliced

125g shiitake mushrooms, sliced

100g bean sprouts

1 tbsp toasted sesame seeds

Method

Heat the oil in a large pan and add the spring onions, cook on a medium heat for 2-3 minutes or until soft. Add the mushrooms and bean sprouts and cook for a further 2-3 minutes, continually stirring. Next add the stock, miso paste and mirin and bring to the boil. Reduce the heat to a gentle simmer then add the tofu and cook for a further five minutes. Ladle into bowls, sprinkle each bowl with toasted sesame seeds and serve.

Liver support boost

Foods that help support liver function include spices such as ginger, fennel, turmeric and garlic, and vegetables such as celery, onions, leeks and chicory also known as endive. Try this quick salad designed to help support liver function.

Celery and chicory salad

Serves 4

Ingredients

1 head chicory, sliced

1 head of chicory, leaves removed whole

2 stalks of celery, chopped

100g lamb's lettuce

120g goat's cheese

50g pecan nuts

Dressing

1tsp Dijon mustard

50ml white wine vinegar

150ml olive oil

Salt and pepper

Method

Start by making the dressing by combining the vinegar and mustard and then gradually add the olive oil. Season to taste with salt and freshly ground pepper. Pour the dressing into a jar and cover. You will have made more dressing than you need but it keeps well in the fridge. Next, combine the sliced chicory, celery and lamb's lettuce and transfer to a serving dish. Sprinkle over the dressing to taste and then crumble the goat's cheese over the leaves and sprinkle with the pecan nuts. Tuck the whole chicory leaves around edge of dish and it's ready to serve. Serve the remainder of the dressing in a side dish or jar.

Tryptophan boost

Foods rich in tryptophan include egg whites, turkey, fish, cottage cheese, yoghurt, peanuts, oats, avocados and pumpkin seeds

Turkey snack

Serves 1 or 2 depending on how hungry you are!

Ingredients

2 oat cakes

¼ avocado

1 slice of good quality turkey breast

2 tsp cottage cheese

Black pepper

Method

Divide the avocado quarter between the two oat cakes spreading it like you would butter. Next, split the turkey slice in half and layer on top of the avocado. Next place a teaspoon of cottage cheese on top of the turkey slice. Add a screw of black pepper and serve.

Moreish Bespoke Catering

Founded in 2006 by Claudine Allen, Moreish Bespoke Catering has experience in catering for a wide range of food styles from rustic feasts to decadent gourmet canapés. Influenced by her Lebanese and English background, combined with a culturally mixed upbringing in Sierra Leone and Belgium, Claudine continues to follow her lifelong passion for food and flavours. Claudine now focuses on freelance chefing, creating bespoke menus and nutritional recipes for private clients. For more info visit www.moreish.co.uk or contact Claudine on 07793547124 or email info@moreish.co.uk.

Help List

Health Tests

Genova Testing Laboratory

Parkgate House, 356 West Barnes Lane, New Malden, Surrey, KT3 6NB
Tel: 020 8336 7750
www.gdx.uk.net

Nutrition

Biocare

Lakeside, 180 Lifford Lane, Kings Norton, Birmingham, B30 3NU
www.biocare.co.uk

The British Association of Nutritional Therapists (BANT)

Email: theadministrator@bant.org.uk
www.bant.org.uk

Higher Nature

Burwash Common, East Sussex, TN19 7LX
Tel: 01435 883484
Email: info@higher-nature.co.uk
www.higher-nature.co.uk

Nurturing Spirit Ltd

Susie Perry Debice
Email: susie@nurturingspirit.co.uk
www.nurturingspirit.co.uk

Nutri-link

Nutrition House, 24 Milber Trading Estate, Newton Abbot, Devon, TQ12 4SG
Tel: 08450 760 402
www.nutri-linkltd.co.uk

Nutri Ltd

Meridian House, Botany Business Park, Macclesfield Road, Whaley Bridge,
High Peak, SK23 7DQ
Tel: 0800 212 742
Email: nutrition@nutri.co.uk
www.nutri-online.co.uk

Vegetarian Society

Parkdale, Dunham Road, Altrincham, Cheshire, WA14 4QG
Tel: 0161 925 2000
Email: info@vegsoc.org
www.vegsoc.org

Acupuncture

The British Acupuncture Council (BAcC)

63 Jeddo Road, London, W12 9HQ
Tel: 020 8735 0400
www.acupuncture.org.uk

Elaine Cook

Dyke Road Natural Health Clinic, 274 Dyke Road, Brighton, BN1 5AE
Tel: 01273 561845
www.ecacupuncture.co.uk

Homeopathy

Ainsworths Homeopathic Pharmacy

36 New Cavendish Street, London , W1G 8UF
Tel: 020 7935 5330
Email: london@ainsworths.com
www.ainsworths.com

Helios Homeopathic Pharmacy

89-97 Camden Rd, Tunbridge Wells, Kent, TN1 2QR
Tel: 01892 537254
Email: pharmacy@helios.co.uk
www.helios.co.uk

Lisa Bullen

The Society of Homeopaths
11 Brookfield, Duncan Close, Moulton Park, Northampton, NN3 6WL
Tel: 0845 450 6611
www.homeopathy-soh.org

Nelson's Homeopathy

Nelson's House, 83 Parkside, London SW1P 5LP
Tel: 020 7629 3118
Email: pharmacy@nelsons.net
www.nelsonshomeopathy.com

Aromatherapy

The International Federation of Aromatherapists (IFA)

20A The Mall, Ealing Broadway, London, W5 2PJ
Tel 020 8567 2243/020 8567 1923
www.ifaroma.org

Laura Hoy

Tel 07828954020
laura@laurahoy.com

New Directions

Unit 19, Sandleheath Industrial Estate, Fordingbridge, Hampshire, SP6 1PA
Tel: 01425 655555
Email: info@newdirectionsUK.com
www.newdirectionsuk.com

NHR Organic Oils

24 Chatham Place, Brighton, BN1 3TN
Tel: 0845 310 8066
Email: info@nhrorganicoils.com
www.nhrorganicoils.com

Quinessence Aromatherapy

Forest Court, Linden Way, Coalville, Leicestershire LE67 3JY
Tel: 01530 835918
Email: support@quinessence.com
www.quinessence.com

Tisserand Oils

Customer Service, First Natural Brands Ltd., Newtown Road, Hove, Sussex, BN3 7BA
Tel: 01273 325 666
Email: sales@tisserand.com
www.tisserand.com

Flower Essences

Australian Bush Flower Essences

45 Booralie Road, Terrey Hills, NSW 2084, Australia
Tel: 00 612 9450 1388
www.ausflowers.com.au

Bach Flower Remedies

Mount Vernon, Bakers Lane, Brightwell-cum-Sotwell, Oxon, OX10 0PZ
Tel: 01491 834678
www.bachcentre.com

The British Flower and Vibrational Essences Association (BFVEA)

London, WC1N 3XX
Tel: 01308 458 784
www.bfvea.com

Findhorn Flower Essence

Cullerne House, Findhorn, Forres, Morayshire, IV36 3YY
Tel: 01309 690 129
Email: sales@findhornessences.com
www.findhornessences.com

Living Tree Orchid Essences

International Flower Essence Repertoire (IFER), Isle of Gigha, Argyll, Scotland, PA41 7AD
Tel: 01583 505400
www.healingorchids.com

Natural Hormones

Dr Lisa McCready

lisamccready@mac.com

Receptura Pharmaproduktion GmbH

FIZ Frankfurter Innovationszentrum Biotechnologie, Uni-Campus Riedberg,
Altenhöferallee 3, D-60438, Frankfurt am Main
Tel: +49 (0) 69 92 880-300
Email: info@receptura.de
www.receptura.de

Life coaching

Mark Shields

Life Practice UK, The Health Station Private Clinic, 21A Brand Street, Hitchin,
Hertfordshire, SG5 1JE
Tel: 01462 451473
Email: info@lifepractice.co.uk
www.lifepractice.co.uk

Relationship counselling

Relate

Helpline Tel: 0300 100 1234
www.relate.org.uk